HARTFORD MAYOR
Ann Uccello

HARTFORD MAYOR
Ann Uccello
— *A Connecticut Trailblazer* —

PAUL PIRROTTA
Foreword by Dennis House

THE History PRESS

Published by The History Press
Charleston, SC
www.historypress.net

Back cover, lower right: Ann Uccello's collection.

First published 2015

Manufactured in the United States

ISBN 978.1.46711.889.7

Library of Congress Control Number: 2015947045

Notice: The information in this book is true and complete to the best of our knowledge. It is offered without guarantee on the part of the author or The History Press. The author and The History Press disclaim all liability in connection with the use of this book.

To all immigrants and, especially, to the Italians in the Hartford area for the sacrifice and hard work that have made it possible for all future generations to live the American dream.

Contents

Foreword

As one walks through the downtown of one of the oldest cities in America, there are reminders of the many leaders this city has had. There is Pratt Street, named for Francis Pratt, the founder of a machine tool making company that led to today's Pratt and Whitney company, the United Technologies subsidiary that makes jet engines. There is the Bulkeley Bridge, named for Morgan Bulkeley, a mayor of Hartford, a governor of Connecticut, a U.S. senator and later a commissioner of Major League Baseball who was inducted into the baseball Hall of Fame in Cooperstown.

There is also a small street that links Bushnell Park to the city's North End that bears a name that might be mispronounced: Ann Uccello Street. Where does the woman for whom this street is named fit into the history of the city of Hartford?

As a young reporter for the CBS station in Hartford, I once noticed a wall of photographs inside city hall of all the people who had served as mayor of Hartford, or at least all of those who served after photography was invented. Man after man after man was mayor from 1774 until 1967, when history was made and a woman was elected mayor of Hartford.

I met Antonina Uccello in the 1990s and liked her instantly. She reminded me of my favorite Italian aunt, and I was fascinated by her stories of what it was like to be a woman in charge in the *Mad Men* era. Shortly after she was elected, Uccello told me she was still asked to get coffee for some of the men in city hall.

Mayor Uccello's election made news around the nation. There had been one or two other women in the United States elected mayor before, but she was the first of a capital city, a political event that made newspaper headlines as far away as Moscow—"America Elects Woman." What must have the Soviets thought?

Mayor Uccello was a calming influence during the riots that plagued Hartford in the late 1960s as they did elsewhere in the country. Her warm no-nonsense demeanor helped unite a city torn apart by racial unrest, the Vietnam War and the assassinations of Martin Luther King and Robert Kennedy.

The popular mayor was reelected and was instantly seen as a candidate for higher office, attracting the attention of President Nixon and the Republican National Committee.

In this book you'll learn about this trailblazer whose name is familiar to tens of thousands of drivers who see the highway signs directing them to the street that bears her name and no doubt say, "Who is Ann Uccello?"

—DENNIS HOUSE

Named one of the "12 Most Influential People" by *Hartford Magazine*, *Eyewitness News* anchor and *Face the State* moderator Dennis House has been a mainstay on local news since 1992. He is a family friend of Ann Uccello.

Preface

When she said yes, it was a dream come true!

No, I am not referring to the marriage proposal to my wife, which obviously also ranks up there, but rather to the request that I be allowed to write a book about Antonina "Ann" Uccello, mayor of Hartford from 1967 to 1971 and, as important in my eyes, the daughter of immigrants from the same home city in Sicily, Canicattini Bagni, where I was born and which I left for Hartford in August 1970.

And just like a marriage proposal, the road to this rendezvous was as tortuous and as unexpected as it was improbable.

From my arrival in Hartford to now, 2015, as I write this book, I spent most of my career in banking. Following my retirement and with grandchildren on the horizon, I began to feel the need to document where we came from, how we grew up, our holidays, our sports, our schooling. I wanted to leave my grandchildren a written account of life in Sicily before our coming to America. In 2009, I published *From Sicily to Connecticut*, an account of the first twenty years of my life in Sicily and the next forty years in the United States.

Armed with time on my hands and a desire never before really felt to preserve our Italian heritage and the history of Italian immigration to the Hartford area, I created a website, Casa Emigranti Italiani (House of the Italian Immigrants), and began collecting stories and pictures from people who, like me, had left their homes to come to Hartford.

Over the past several years, the site has accumulated hundreds of personal stories and historical accounts of the challenges faced by the early immigrants. It also contains the historical account of the neighborhoods that became the Little Italy of Hartford, with a special focus on the legendary Front Street, which had been home to thousands of Italians, as well as immigrants from other countries, and was razed in 1960 in the name of urban renewal to make room for a plaza that sits empty in the middle of unused office space.

In 2012, I saw an article in the local paper that intrigued me: Antonina "Ann" Uccello, former mayor of Hartford, had turned ninety and was being presented the key to the city by the present mayor, Pedro Segarra.

I figured, incorrectly as it turned out, that Ms. Uccello could be a great source of information about Front Street, as I assumed that her parents would have settled there. In the fall of 2012, I sent a letter asking to meet her so that I could interview her and mentioned my website and interest in Front Street.

I received no response for several months, but one afternoon my cellphone rang, and a vibrant voice on the end of the line told me that I was speaking to former mayor Uccello. I literally almost fell off my chair. We had a very pleasant conversation (she explained to me that her family had never lived in the Front Street area and hence that was the reason she had not called me earlier), and I asked Ann if we could meet and if I could bring with me a very special guest, Paolo Amenta, mayor of Canicattini Bagni, the birthplace of both her parents. He was in Hartford for the 2013 Columbus Day festivities and wanted to meet her.

Several days later, Mayor Amenta; Ann; her nephew David Gustafson; and his wife, Jacqui; and I had lunch at the retirement community where Ann lives. What a fantastic experience for both Mayor Amenta and myself—the honor to have had the pleasure of spending a few hours with Ninetta (as her mother would call her, an abbreviation of the first name Antonina).

Two things jumped at me from that visit: Ann could speak our Sicilian dialect as well as any of us, and at ninety-one, her mind was as sharp as any fifty-year-old person.

Our next contact was in the winter of 2014. I was organizing a pictorial exhibit on the history of Italian immigration into the Hartford area and asked if she could contribute some pictures and also attend the grand opening ceremony, which was going to also feature Mayor Segarra. She agreed to both requests, and the exhibition was that much richer for it.

As I did my research about Italian Americans in general and Ann's political career in particular, I came to a finding that surprised me: no one had ever written a book about her life story.

Mayor Amenta, Mayor Uccello and the author in 2013. *Author's collection.*

When I arrived in Hartford in 1970, Ann was the pride of our Italian community, a woman and a Republican who somehow had managed to win back-to-back mayoral elections in Hartford, a city where Republicans were outnumbered by Democrats by a three-to-one ratio. She is, in fact, a historical figure: the first female mayor in the city of Hartford, the first female mayor in the state of Connecticut and the first woman in the entire country to be elected mayor of a capital city. And yet no one had bothered to contact her to document this incredible life.

After mulling over the idea, I popped the question: would Ann allow me to work with her to document her life story?

I am exaggerating only slightly in stating that when Ann said yes, I felt like the happiest man in the world. I feel a special bond to this woman because of her parents and the home city we share, and I feel privileged to have been chosen to document the remarkable life of a trailblazer, a compassionate conservative long before the term ever existed.

Starting in June 2014, we met twice a week at her residence. We would have lunch in the cafeteria, sharing a sandwich, or once in a while I would bring some Italian delicacies like *umbanata* (spinach pie), pizza, cookies and cannolis. But not too often, and not all at the same time; health and age only allow so much splurging.

We would spend between two and three hours per session in her apartment, where I would ask questions and tape our discussion. Ann also made available to me all kinds of pictures and countless other documents, which I supplemented with newspaper articles of the times.

In addition to my time with Ann, I have also been able to spend time with her sisters Nellie and Carmela; with Carmela's son, David; with Ann's campaign manager, George Ducharme; and with her policy advisor, Judge Dick Rittenband.

This is not a political book, and it is not designed to address the political or policy issues of the day. It is an effort to document Ann's life, her persona and her family.

The more time I spend learning about her life, her family, about the challenges she faced and conquered, the more proud I am of the Italian American heritage we share and at being given the opportunity to write this book. I feel like one of the family.

The reaction to my efforts when I share the project with my friends has been interesting. The first reaction has been almost unanimously: "Is she still alive?" When I assure them that at ninety-three as of this writing, Ann is not only alive but also still has as sharp a mind as ever, their second reaction is: "She was the last great mayor."

I hope you enjoy this book as much as I have enjoyed working on it.

Introduction

In April 2014, Mayor Segarra of Hartford was speaking to a crowd gathered to celebrate the grand opening of an exhibition on the immigration of Italians to Hartford when he turned to his left and broke into the wide grin you reserve for those occasions when, suddenly and unexpectedly, you see your best friend walk into the room. "Madame Mayor," he exclaimed, "I was not aware that you would be here." Antonina "Ann" Uccello, mayor of Hartford from 1967 to 1971, had just joined the opening ceremony.

"Uccello Denies She Is a Politician" glared the headline in the 1967 *Hartford Courant*, but as the article points out, it would have been very hard to convince her vanquished opponents. A conservative Republican in a city where Democrats, led by the legendary State and National Party chairman John Bailey, held a three-to-one advantage in voter registration, Ann achieved the impossible: she became the first ever female mayor in the history of Hartford, the first female mayor in the history of the state, the first woman in the entire country to be elected mayor of a major city and the last Republican to occupy that position in Hartford.

In many ways, her success story is not unlike that of many second-generation Italian Americans who overcame discrimination, ignorance and a humble beginning to achieve the American dream—with some major exceptions. A woman born in the 1920s was not supposed to focus on her career while choosing to remain single, was not supposed to enter politics and was not supposed to be a Republican.

Her parents were part of the wave of millions of Italian immigrants who came to the United States between 1900 and 1925. Her father, Salvatore Uccello, arrived in 1907. In 1920, he went back to the small city in Southeast Sicily from where he originated to marry Ann's mother, Josephine Bordonaro. It was an arranged marriage, as was the custom back in those days, but unusual in that the bride's father "recruited" the groom while on a trip to the United States.

The immigrant's story of Ann's parents follows a familiar pattern. The father worked long hours as a shoemaker to support the family while the mother remained home to take care of the children. They lived in Hartford all their lives but never in the Italian East Side of Front Street.

Losses in the stock market crash of 1929 led to the closing of the shop and semi-frequent moves from apartment to apartment. But after a brief period of time, Salvatore reopened the shop, and the family fortunes improved. Four of the five girls went on to graduate from college.

Life inside the Uccello household was never dull. Friends and relatives would come and go. Sunday afternoons would see the girls stage talent shows for their parents and visitors. From time to time, boys would also be the subject of discussion. Ann recalls one particular night when the five girls and their mother were sitting around the kitchen table gossiping about this and that boy and how not one of them measured up to the Uccello daughters. After several minutes of listening to this nonsense from another room, her father, usually a meek and kind person who did not speak much, came to the kitchen and admonished them, saying, "What are you expecting, Michelangelo to come down and paint you one? Remember, you are not all that perfect yourselves." Then he went back to his room, leaving everyone stunned and silent.

Carmela was the prettiest of the sisters, and the boys tended to swarm around her. But the five girls were not the only attraction to the Uccello home—their mother's cooking was a close competitor, and a dinner invitation was a much sought-after honor. Literally hundreds would be invited over for dinner during Ann's political years.

Ann grew into a socially conscious woman interested in politics and social issues, an interest she cultivated by registering with the Republican Party and taking part in campaign events while also helping with administrative work within the party. She did so at the expense of her personal social life. Dating was not a top priority, and suitors were never encouraged. She would never marry, a choice driven by her belief that doing so would inhibit or limit her outside activities and that it was not fair to the other person if she had to spend much of her time outside the family. Her decision perhaps was also influenced by the life of her mother: a dedicated housewife who never did much outside the home and only late in life got a chance to experience the excitement of life in Washington, D.C.

In 1940, Ann was accepted at Saint Joseph College (now the University of Saint Joseph), and in 1944, she became the first member of her family to graduate. She would have preferred to attend Central Connecticut College to become a teacher, but her father demanded that she attend a Catholic college. Saint Joseph, a nearby college established in 1932 by the Sisters of Mercy of Connecticut, became the logical choice. Her attendance there started a relationship between the Uccello family and the school that lasts to this day. Ann's elder sister Vincenza graduated from and eventually became a professor and the first art history director at the school, and sister Nellie graduated in 1954, along with cousin Nellie Agostino and several other relatives.

College strengthened the values Ann's parents had instilled in her while at the same time encouraged her to pursue her dreams and to reject any artificial limitations on what she could accomplish in life.

Following graduation, Ann got a teaching job at the East Hampton High School, and it turned out to be far more of a challenge than expected. It turned out teaching was not her calling.

In 1945, Ann began a new job search, unsure of where her future was heading. She received a job offer from Aetna, one of the many large insurance companies that dotted the Harford landscape, and another offer from G. Fox and Co., which she accepted. During the next fifteen-plus years, Ann's social life mainly consisted of three activities: work as a volunteer at Saint Joseph College in the newly established alumni office, volunteer work in the Catholic Graduates Club and volunteer activities with the local Hartford Young Republicans. Dating was minimal, but she developed a friendship with two G. Fox colleagues, George Ducharme and Mary Barry, who would have a major influence in her life.

In 1963, Ann fought her way into a slot on the New Republican Party ticket for the Hartford Town Council, and much to her surprise—and that of everyone else—she placed seventh out of a roster of nineteen. It would be only the first of the many political surprises Ann would pull off over the next eight years.

Chapter 1

The Parents' Story

Ann's father, Salvatore, was born in 1890, the son of Vincenza and Sebastiano Uccello. Giuseppina "Josephine" Bordonaro was born in 1900, the daughter of Gaetano Bordonaro and Filomena Vasquez. Josephine was the youngest, while Salvatore was the eldest of four brothers, all of whom would immigrate to the United States, and three sisters, one of whom, Lucy, also would come to America.

Mr. and Mrs. Uccello were born in Canicattini Bagni, a small hill city near Siracusa, in the southeastern-most part of Sicily. One of the smallest cities in the county in terms of land area, Canicattini's population grew from 5,200 in 1861 to 11,800 in 1921 and has since decreased steadily to 7,000 in 2015.

Mr. Uccello came from a poor family while Josephine's parents were fairly well-to-do landowners who lived in a palazzo ("palace") in the downtown center of the small city. In those days, it was as rare to see a marriage between two people from different classes as it was to see a marriage between people of different cities.

Salvatore first came to America in 1907 (at least, this appears to be the date from research of the Ellis Island records), one of the five million Italians who immigrated to the United States between 1880 and 1925. Of these Italian immigrants, 80 percent were from the south of Italy.

Economic conditions in Italy, a country that had just fought a war of unification culminating in 1870 with the Kingdom of Italy, were disastrous, and especially so in the south. Emigration was the answer, and Italians began to leave by the hundreds of thousands for places like America, Argentina, Canada and Brazil.

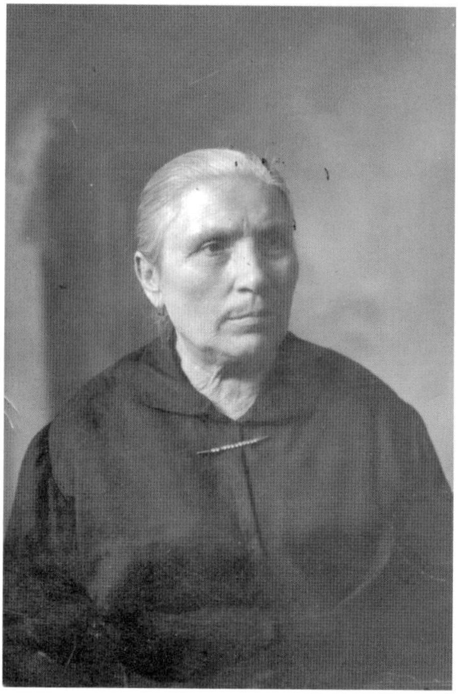

Left: Gaetano Bordonaro, Ann's maternal grandfather. *Ann Uccello's collection.*

Right: Filomena Bordonaro, Ann's maternal grandmother. *Ann Uccello's collection.*

Agriculture was the largest component of the economy in Sicily and in Canicattini, but the social and lifestyle gap between landowners, who had survived the feudal system, and the day laborers was as large as a canyon. Large families were the norm (with male children preferred), and children would begin backbreaking work from a very young age. Men would leave home for weeks at a time to harvest the oranges, olives and wheat that would be presented to the landowners in exchange for food (until the early 1950s, it was not uncommon to pay the barber in grain) and a meager cash pay, if any. Most children would either not attend school at all or attend school only until second or third grade. Illiteracy was rampant.

The town also had a fairly large group of tradesmen consisting of the shoemakers (such as Salvatore's father), tailors, barbers and the famed *murassiccari*, experienced workers who built walls (*muro*) all in a dry (*a siccu*) system that used no mortar or any other aid. Such were the skills of these individuals that the walls they built stand to this day.

Left: Sebastiano Uccello, Ann's paternal grandfather. *Ann Uccello's collection.*

Right: Vincenza Uccello, Ann's paternal grandmother. *Ann Uccello's collection.*

Some of these workers were artists: many a home still features an architectural style called Liberty, which saw in Canicattini its finest examples, including detailed sculptures in stone, produced with a hammer and chisel and nothing else. Nowhere is this work more visible than in the local cemetery, where the well-to-do commissioned the famed Cappellas, a family burial chapel that featured on its exterior some of the finest stonework details, almost as ornate as a *barocco* church.

Most emigrants left with the intent to save money and return to their home countries to buy land and live well. But reality has a way of intruding on plans, and a large number remained and created Italian colonies, such as the one on the Hartford East Side.

Salvatore had been a very religious person from early in life and had actually spent several years studying for the priesthood, which made him a very educated young man, very much an exception in those days. He immigrated to the United States in 1907, at first settling in Salem, Massachusetts, before moving to Hartford, Connecticut.

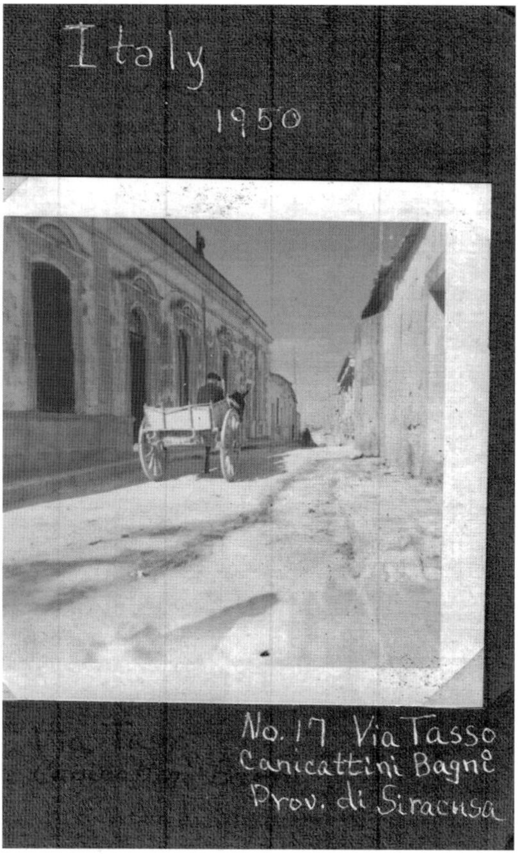

Canicattini, Torquato Tasso Street, where Ann's parents were born. *Ann Uccello's collection.*

On June 25, 1914, a devastating fire ignited on Boston Street in Blubber Hollow, the leather-manufacturing district of Salem. Over the course of two days, this massive fire destroyed 1,376 buildings and left eighteen thousand people, almost half of Salem's population, homeless and many without jobs. With an uncle, Salvatore moved to Hartford, where he took up the shoemaker trade he had learned back home from his father.

In 1920, he went back to the small city in Southeast Sicily from which he originated to marry Ann's mother, Josephine Bordonaro. It was an arranged marriage, as was the custom back in those days, but unusual in that the bride's father "recruited" the groom while on a trip to the United States.

His marriage to Josephine was also unusual in at least one other way: the bride's family was well-to-do, patrician landowners—one member of the family even served as mayor of the small city—while Salvatore's family consisted of poor tradesmen (Salvatore's father was also a shoemaker) who performed long hours of backbreaking work for not much more than basic sustenance. Salvatore was a loving parent, a strict disciplinarian (Ann could not attend her senior ball because she would have had to stay out past midnight, and her father refused to bend the rules) and an extremely religious person who started every day by going to early Mass.

A meek and humble person, Salvatore valued education, and unlike many of his contemporaries, he encouraged his daughters to attend college—although, at least in Ann's case, it had to be a Catholic college.

Right: The cemetery chapel in Canicattini shows the rich details of the work done by the sculptors. *Author's collection.*

Below: Views of Canicattini from a postcard from the 1960s. *Courtesy Carpinteri Printing.*

Josephine devoted her life to her husband and their five daughters. Her cooking was legendary, and she was a good seamstress who could turn some inexpensive material into an acceptable dress or skirt. She loved to be the center of attention, and she was the life of the party. In many ways, when Ann entered politics, her mother became Ann's principal political advisor. By contrast, Ann's father, afflicted by poor health, was largely hands-off in his daughter's political career.

Ann's father was a hardworking man, dedicated to his family, church and clients. Until his retirement in 1954, he worked six days a week from early in the morning to late at night. Sometimes he ate lunch at home if business was slow, but on most occasions, his lunch was delivered to the shop by Ann or one of her sisters.

Salvatore started the day at Mass before going to work, and every Sunday, the entire family would occupy a pew in the front of the church. Salvatore became very close to the clergy, who would later help him and his family during the Great Depression.

For over twenty years, Salvatore's shop was located at the corner of Garden and Homestead Avenues, but prior to that, he headed the first shoe repairs department at G. Fox. Who could imagine that twenty-five years later Ann would go to work at G. Fox and become a close collaborator of Mrs. Auerbach, the owner, whose permission she would seek to run for office.

Ann's parents took one real vacation in their entire lives. In 1954, Salvatore and Josephine traveled to Italy and then on to Sicily for their only other joint visit to their birthplace since their return in 1927 (more on this later).

Josephine's life was less eventful than Salvatore's, and in some ways, one could argue that coming to America for her was a sacrifice and that life in Canicattini as the member of a prominent and well-to-do family would have been just fine. Salvatore and Josephine would not have met had it not been for her father, Gaetano Bordonaro, a bon vivant who is famous for coming to the United States and, when asked how he liked it, answering, "I don't like it. All they do is work." But that visit to Hartford in late 1916 or 1917 produced one substantial benefit: Bordonaro met a young Salvatore Uccello and was so impressed that he invited him to visit Canicattini and meet his daughter Josephine.

In 1920, Salvatore did just that, and later that year, he and Josephine were married and moved to Hartford. Vincenza was born in 1921, Antonina in 1922, Carmela in 1926, Virgilia in 1929 and Sebastiana in 1932. One can only imagine the trepidation of Josephine at marrying

Left: Salvatore Uccello, Ann's father, in the 1920s. *Ann Uccello's collection.*

Right: Josephine Uccello, Ann's mother, in a 1927 picture. *Ann Uccello's collection.*

a relatively unknown man and leaving the comfort of home to face the challenges of a new land. Fortunately, Salvatore's sister Lucy decided to come to Hartford with the Uccellos, and that may have been a godsend. Lucy would be as much a sister to Josephine as she was to Salvatore, and she helped at home with the children.

The home and family were the main focus of Josephine's life. She took care of her family and the house, cooked up a storm and otherwise had no diversions. She did belong to the Principessa Maria Pia Society and took on a semiactive role helping arrange tea parties and supporting the local Columbus Day celebrations.

The invitation to join the Maria Pia society reflects the class separation that existed within the community back home in Italy and had been carried over to the States. By the 1930s, Hartford had a fairly large number of immigrants who called Canicattini home and more kept coming, thus providing a ready source of new members. As was usual in those days, mutual aid societies would be formed for immigrants to assist one another and to aid in the transition to life in a foreign land and with a strange language.

Most of these clubs—and there were literally hundreds of them within Hartford—would be based on the specific city of origin, so there was the Pratolani club for people who came from Pratola Peligna, Abruzzo, and the Floridian Club for people who came from Floridia and so on. These divisions reflected the fractious nature of Italy, where small city states had survived for hundreds of years, where neighboring towns would often be at "war" with one another, where strangers were looked at with suspicion and where marriages between people from different towns were frowned upon.

The Daughters of Canicattinesi Society was formed in 1936 and still exists to this day. It had hundreds of members, and all of the members were either born in Canicattini or were born here in Hartford from parents who hailed from Canicattini. Members of this society were largely of the working class.

In 1937, a group of women also hailing from Canicattini formed the Principessa Maria Pia Society, named after the heiress to the house of Savoy, which, in those days, ruled Italy. Membership was much more selective, and it represented the upper class among the immigrants. Given Josephine's background, she was invited to join the Maria Pia Society.

A member of a politically prominent family, Josephine would bring her political skills to bear on her daughter's political campaigns, participating fully in campaign strategy meetings held around the dining room table of their Branford Street home. She encouraged her daughters to seek higher education as a means of leading more meaningful and fulfilling lives.

Late evenings would find mother and daughters discussing art, child psychology, literature, current events, politics and operas, many of which Josephine knew by heart and sang with the exuberance of a soprano diva. A dynamic and gracious hostess, she enjoyed entertaining, was a superb cook and extended her warm and generous hospitality to all who came to her home.

In 1927, Josephine and the three girls—Vincenza, Ann and Carmela—returned to Sicily. Josephine had developed breathing difficulties, and the doctor felt that a change of air would do her good. And, in fact, as soon as she got on the ship, she started to feel a lot better. They would end up spending about a year and a half in Canicattini, and the two older girls had a chance to attend local schools (Ann can recall to this day in Italian a poem she learned back then). In 1928, their father went to Sicily, and the entire family returned to Hartford shortly thereafter.

Oh yes, the mysterious breathing difficulty experienced by Mrs. Uccello—turned out she was allergic to a dog, Prince, they had acquired for the girls and which the father donated to another family. No dog, no breathing problems.

Left: A 1928 passport page for Salvatore Uccello. *Ann Uccello's collection.*

Right: A 1928 passport picture of Josephine Uccello and Ann, Carmela and Vincenza. *Ann Uccello's collection.*

The Uccellos had five daughters. Ann, the second eldest, recalls spending time at her father's shoemaker shop on Albany Avenue in Hartford helping with paperwork and making deliveries as needed, sometimes late at night and just in time to a client who would wear them that very evening for a special occasion. She could walk at night without fear of crime in those days, she recalls wistfully. Her father was often the target of the unenlightened comments of his male contemporaries, who would taunt him about his five daughters but not one son to carry on the family name, a very important consideration to the men of that generation.

Ann recalls one such evening when one of her father's chauvinistic acquaintances came into the shoe repair shop and, after some small talk, departed with the usual taunt: "What's the matter? You could not produce even one male!" Her father did not reply, but Ann could tell that he was deeply hurt. On the way home that evening, Ann broke the silence, saying, "Don't worry, Daddy. We will make you proud of us. Someday the Uccello name will be remembered."

THE GREAT DEPRESSION WAS NOT kind to anyone, including the Uccello family. Ann recalls her father coming home to announce that he was closing the shop. He had lost it all in the stock market crash, and the family had to relocate. He was devastated and fell into a brief bout of depression, sometimes not leaving home at all. Soon enough, however, he announced that he was reopening the shop, and he began to work on putting behind him that unpleasant experience.

Salvatore would have loved to have a son, but he never was anything but supportive of the aspirations of his five daughters. On the night in 1967 that Ann was elected mayor of Hartford, she found him teary eyed in the kitchen, no doubt enormously proud of what his daughter—a first-generation Italian American and a woman—had been able to accomplish.

Salvatore died in 1969 in the middle of the second election for mayor, which Ann again won. Josephine died in 1995, just short of her ninety-fifth birthday, having witnessed the success of all of her daughters and having enjoyed, at least for a few years, the social life that a job in Washington for daughter Ann brought about.

Ann's political philosophy was formed on this base of hard work, sacrifice and opportunity for all. She was a compassionate conservative well before the term was in vogue.

Chapter 2

Five Sisters and Family Values

Just imagine an apartment in the 1930s: husband, wife, five daughters—and ONE bathroom. Today, there would be a revolution, a war, but in the 1930s and '40s, this was normal. And, of course, this being the 1930s, the father had total control and precedence over the use of the bathroom, as well as everything else in the family. Fortunately, he would leave home early and come back late.

At home, they spoke the Sicilian dialect with their parents and primarily English among themselves—unless they did not want to be understood by others, in which case they would communicate in the dialect.

In many ways, the Uccellos were not your typical Italian immigrant family: they did not live in the Italian east side of Hartford, their friends were mostly Jewish and Irish kids and they did not attend the many festivals and festas organized by the local Italian clubs. But their roots to Italy were and still remain extremely strong. Most of the sisters retained the Italian first name in their lives at a time when it was not fashionable to do so, and long after the death of their parents they still consider themselves the daughters of an "Italian shoemaker immigrant." They have visited Italy and Canicattini Bagni (the home city of their parents, located in Sicily) many times, still keep in touch with some of their relatives and still speak fluent Sicilian.

Each sister developed her own identity, and yet they have remained very close and, unlike many sisters, have managed to avoid the family feuds that are unfortunately so common in families, especially Sicilian families.

Ann and Vincenza in the late 1920s. *Ann Uccello's collection.*

Life in the 1930s and '40s, especially at the Uccello home, was a Spartan one with few of the luxuries that we so take for granted today. But this was also a benefit because it resulted in more quality family time.

In the evenings, the six women would have dinner together, while their father would come home late, have supper and rest from a long day at the shop. On Saturdays, they would listen to the opera broadcast, as both

Salvatore and Josephine were opera lovers, and eventually the entire family would attend presentations at Bushnell Memorial.

But Sundays were very special. Nellie recalled how Sunday afternoons used to be show time at the Uccello home. Ann was the master of ceremonies, Carmela would tap dance, Nellie would read poetry and friends and relatives would join in as well. Sebastiano Vasquez, probably Mr. Uccello's closest friend, was a constant presence, and his singing was as much a part of the show as that of the girls. Salvatore's brothers and sister and their children would also attend and would join the program.

When the girls started working, they contributed their earnings to their mother, who would then give them an allowance as needed. Vincenza went to work when she was seventeen. Ann started work in 1944. They followed this pattern until Ann went to Washington to work in the Nixon administration. The amount of money retained by the girls grew larger as they grew older, but the principle was the same.

Nellie recalled in one of our get-togethers that one payday she had cashed her paycheck, returned home and presented her mother with the cash. She was shocked when her mother informed her that she, Nellie, could now do as the others—i.e., keep the paycheck and contribute a monthly amount toward the common expenses. Nellie had never considered that possibility. She was now "rich," but, of course, with that independence came the responsibility of having to pay for her own clothes and other personal items.

Among the sisters, age determined how close they were with one another. Vincenza and Antonina, being the two eldest, would sleep in the same bed and lived together until Vincenza's death in 2004. Gil and Nellie, the two youngest, also were extremely close, while Carmela, the middle child, would become closest to Nellie Agostino, daughter of her father's sister, Lucy, who had migrated to the States with Salvatore and Josephine.

Vincenza was the perpetual student, Ann the politician, Carmela the family woman, Gil the teacher and Nellie the librarian. But these descriptions greatly simplify the complex life they each led.

Vincenza left high school before graduation to work at Royal Typewriter Co. and bring home a much-needed paycheck to help the family. It wasn't until many years later that she would be able to attend college, but only after passing the high school equivalency test, a fact that she had to display on her resume. It so irked her that she lobbied and convinced the board of education to simply indicate a high school diploma, no matter how it was obtained.

She graduated cum laude from Saint Joseph College and obtained an MALS from Wesleyan University and a master's of fine arts from Villa

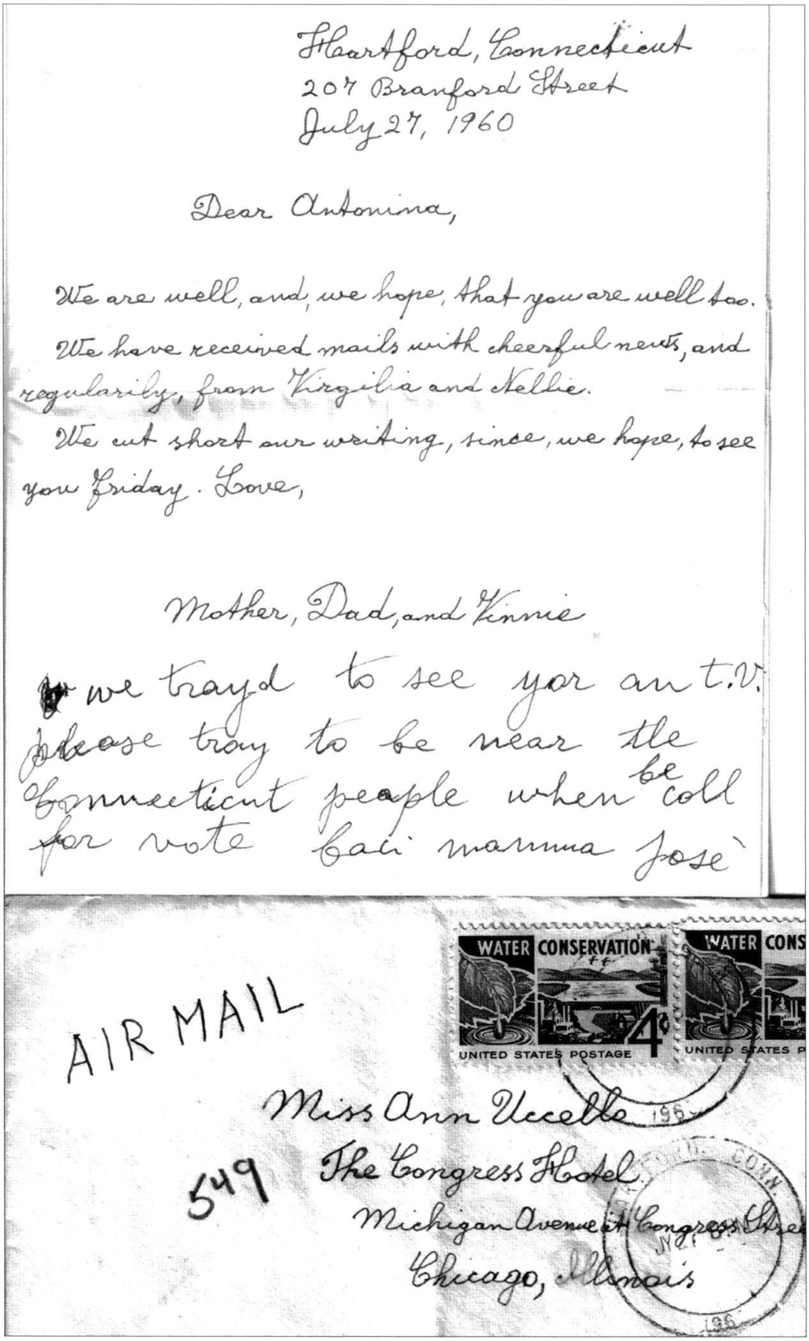

Hartford, Connecticut
207 Branford Street
July 27, 1960

Dear Antonina,

We are well, and, we hope, that you are well too.
We have received mails with cheerful news, and regularily, from Virgilia and Nellie.
We cut short our writing, since, we hope, to see you Friday. Love,

Mother, Dad, and Vinnie

we trayd to see yor an t.v. please tray to be near the Connecticut peaple when be coll for vote Cai mamma Josè

AIR MAIL

WATER CONSERVATION 4¢ UNITED STATES POSTAGE

Miss Ann Uccello
549 The Congress Hotel
Michigan Avenue at Congress Stre
Chicago, Illinois

A 1960 letter from her mother to Ann, who was attending the GOP convention in Chicago. *Ann Uccello's collection.*

Schifanoia Pius XII Institute in Florence, Italy. She left for Italy in 1962 and would be there for eighteen months in what was to become the start of her foreign travel. But this was also the first time that any member of the family would be that far away for such a long period of time. The family was in close touch frequently anyway, with letters and postcards going both directions on a weekly basis to keep everyone updated on things both important and mundane. Vincenza saved many of the letters she received from her mother and sisters, and her family also saved a large number of postcards she sent home from just about every place she visited.

For Vincenza, additional study was a lifetime pursuit done in many different countries and at many different educational institutions, including at Yale University, where she did a visiting faculty fellowship.

In 1964, she started her career at Saint Joseph College, building the fine arts program, serving as the first chair of the department and inspiring her students with knowledge and her enthusiasm for her subject. Her countless college exhibitions enhanced her students' understanding of and appreciation for art. Recognizing the need for galleries to house the college's magnificent art collections, she worked tirelessly to make the dream of an art center a reality. Saint Joseph College honored her in many ways, conferring on her the Distinguished Alumna Award and the title of professor emerita and awarding her the degree of doctor of humane letters, honoris causa. A passionate advocate for the arts, she received the Distinguished Art Advocate Award from the Connecticut Art Education Association in 2002.

Vincenza was a superb artist. Her work in a variety of media and techniques has been displayed in numerous solo, juried and invitational exhibitions throughout Connecticut and the United States. Three of her works were included in "American Painters in Paris," an exhibition held in Paris as a bicentennial tribute to the United States.

After 1977, she concentrated her efforts on the creation of unique and beautiful handmade paper art and received well-deserved acclaim for her work in this medium. Her handmade paper book entitled *A Summer Story* was acquired by the New York Public Library for its rare book collection.

Vincenza made her home for many years with Ann, and the two were extremely close. They traveled overseas together on many occasions, and Ann arranged the cocktail party to celebrate Vincenza's graduation from the Villa Schifanoia program in Florence, Italy. Vincenza left Ann many of the paintings she had authored over the years, paintings that to this day adorn the walls of Ann's apartment.

"Your greatest masterpiece is the mosaic you have fashioned from your artistry, passion and talent. Indeed, your tenure at Saint Joseph College is a work of art whose value is too great to estimate." So states the dedication to Vincenza Agatha Uccello on the occasion of the presentation of the degree of doctor of humane letters, honoris causa, in 2000.

Having five girls ensured a steady stream of suitors or at least "intermediaries," matchmakers who visited the Uccello household to inquire about one of the five. Carmela was the one with the most active dating schedule. She eventually met Russell E. Gustafson Jr. They became engaged in 1951 and married in 1952. Two children, David (1956) and Laura (1961), followed, and Laura would also have two children. The boy was especially welcome in a house where women were the norm. Carmela devoted her life to raising the children, while Russell opened a real estate and insurance business, which Ann would eventually join upon her return from Washington, D.C.

Gil (whose full name, Virgilia, was chosen by her father in honor of the roman poet Virgil) was a 1956 graduate of the Connecticut Teacher College who worked in the Bloomfield school system for many years. She married Alfred Martini in 1968. They lead a quiet life and are alive as of this writing in 2015, but neither is doing too well healthwise.

Nellie showed an interest in writing and the English language from her school days at Jones Junior High. In 1947, she was awarded the Civitan Award Key for good citizenship and was also the editor of the *Northwest Observer*, a highly regarded school paper that received several honors from the prestigious Columbia Scholastic Press Association. In 1949, she was chosen to represent Weaver High School at the annual good citizenship award dinner sponsored each year by the National Society of the Daughters of the American Revolution.

In June 1950, Nellie delivered the valedictorian address at the Weaver High School graduating ceremony. The title was: "Where Do We Go from Here?" Nellie enrolled at Saint Joseph College and, in 1952, became the editor of its paper. In 1955, she became an English teacher at South Windsor High School and married fellow schoolteacher Stephen Romaine in 1962. They remained together until his passing in 2006.

Ann, now ninety-three at this writing and the "matriarch" of the family, adores her sisters almost as much as she does her parents. She is pained by the ravages of time that have visited her sisters: Gil is in a coma-like status, unresponsive and unable to recognize or communicate, while her husband, Al, is now showing the full symptoms of Alzheimer and deteriorating quickly.

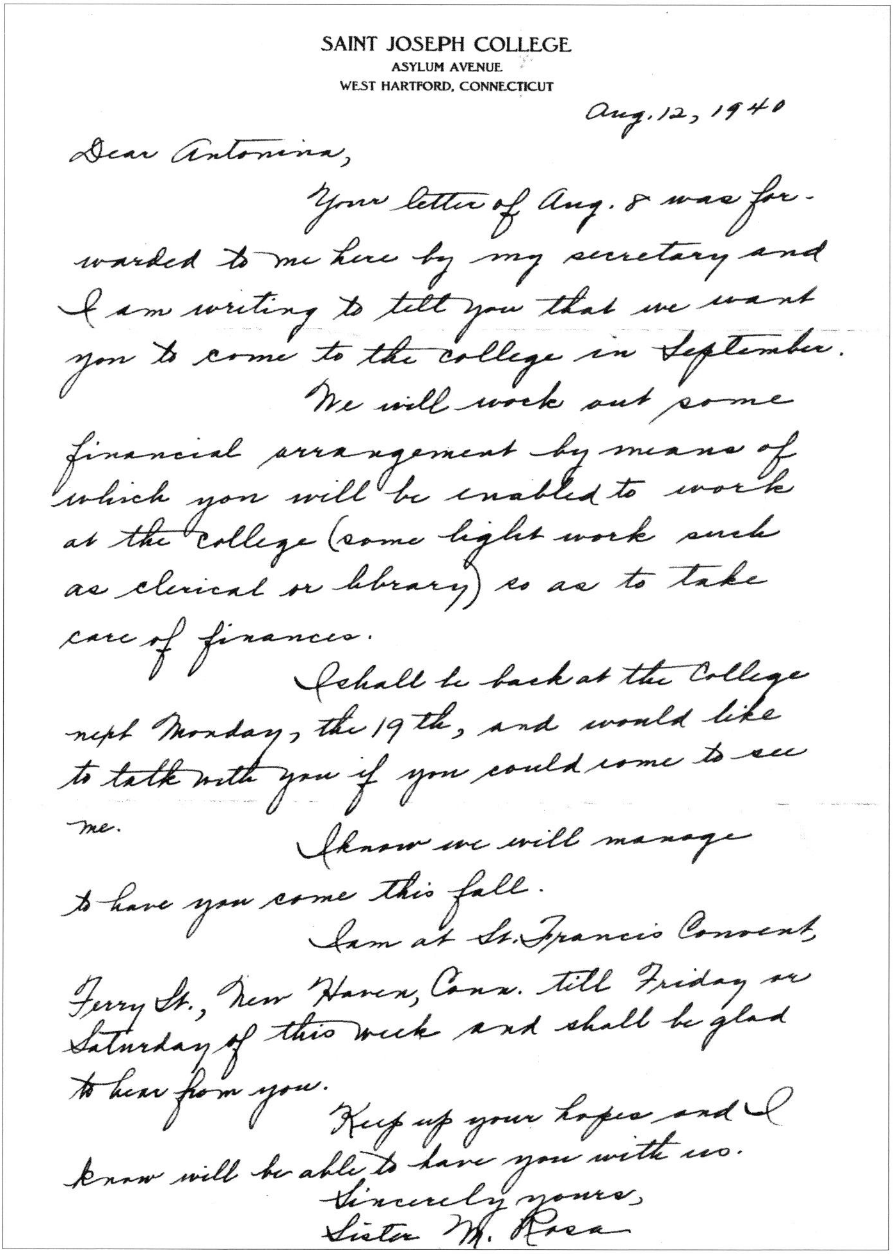

SAINT JOSEPH COLLEGE
ASYLUM AVENUE
WEST HARTFORD, CONNECTICUT

Aug. 12, 1940

Dear Antonina,

Your letter of Aug. 8 was forwarded to me here by my secretary and I am writing to tell you that we want you to come to the college in September.

We will work out some financial arrangement by means of which you will be enabled to work at the college (some light work such as clerical or library) so as to take care of finances.

I shall be back at the College next Monday, the 19th, and would like to talk with you if you could come to see me.

I know we will manage to have you come this fall.

I am at St. Francis Convent, Ferry St., New Haven, Conn. till Friday or Saturday of this week and shall be glad to hear from you.

Keep up your hopes and I know will be able to have you with us.

Sincerely yours,
Sister M. Rosa

A 1940 letter from Sister Rosa at Saint Joseph College, notifying Ann of her admission to college. *Ann Uccello's collection.*

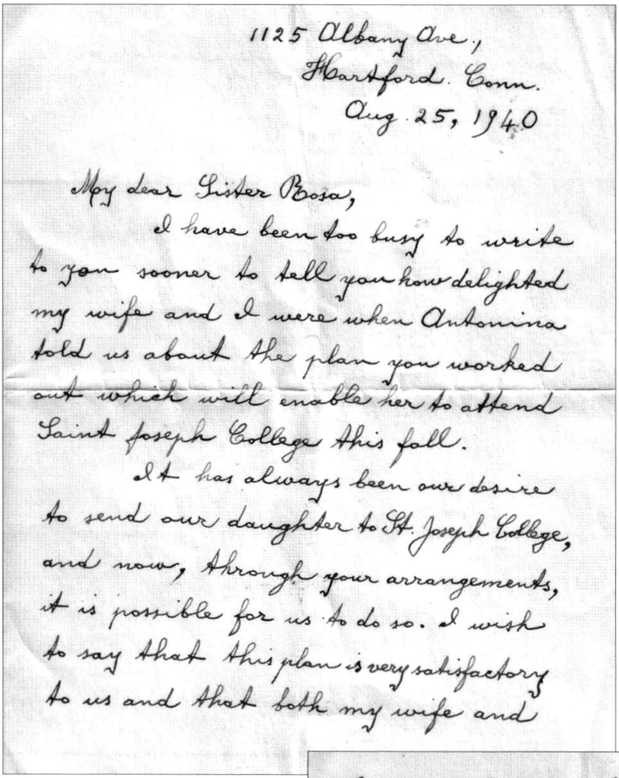

1125 Albany Ave.,
Hartford. Conn.
Aug. 25, 1940

My dear Sister Rosa,

I have been too busy to write to you sooner to tell you how delighted my wife and I were when Antonina told us about the plan you worked out which will enable her to attend Saint Joseph College this fall.

It has always been our desire to send our daughter to St. Joseph College, and now, through your arrangements, it is possible for us to do so. I wish to say that this plan is very satisfactory to us and that both my wife and

Page one of a letter from a grateful Mr. Uccello to Sister Rosa, thanking the sister for her confidence in the family. *Ann Uccello's collection.*

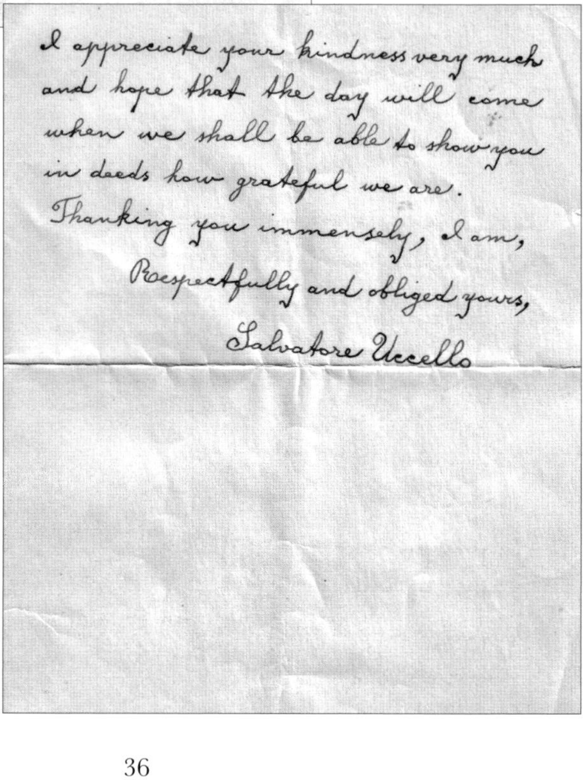

I appreciate your kindness very much and hope that the day will come when we shall be able to show you in deeds how grateful we are.

Thanking you immensely, I am,

Respectfully and obliged yours,

Salvatore Uccello

Page two of the letter to Sister Rosa from Mr. Uccello. *Ann Uccello's collection.*

Russell and Carmela, both eighty-eight, live in the same Avon home they built in 1963, and while still driving, they need more help from David, who is the "supervisor" of all the sisters. Aging is treating the Uccellos not unlike it does many other families.

Josephine's life was not one that Ann would have chosen for herself, and perhaps this is part of the reason why Ann decided to remain single. She felt that she could not do the things she wanted to do and also commit to a life at home and a family—at least not in the same way her mother did, which to her was the only way.

Her choice of a single life was not a whimsical, last-minute decision. In 1936, Ann wrote a school assignment called "My Autobiography." A five-page manuscript, the last chapter is titled "My Future." It states, "Like my

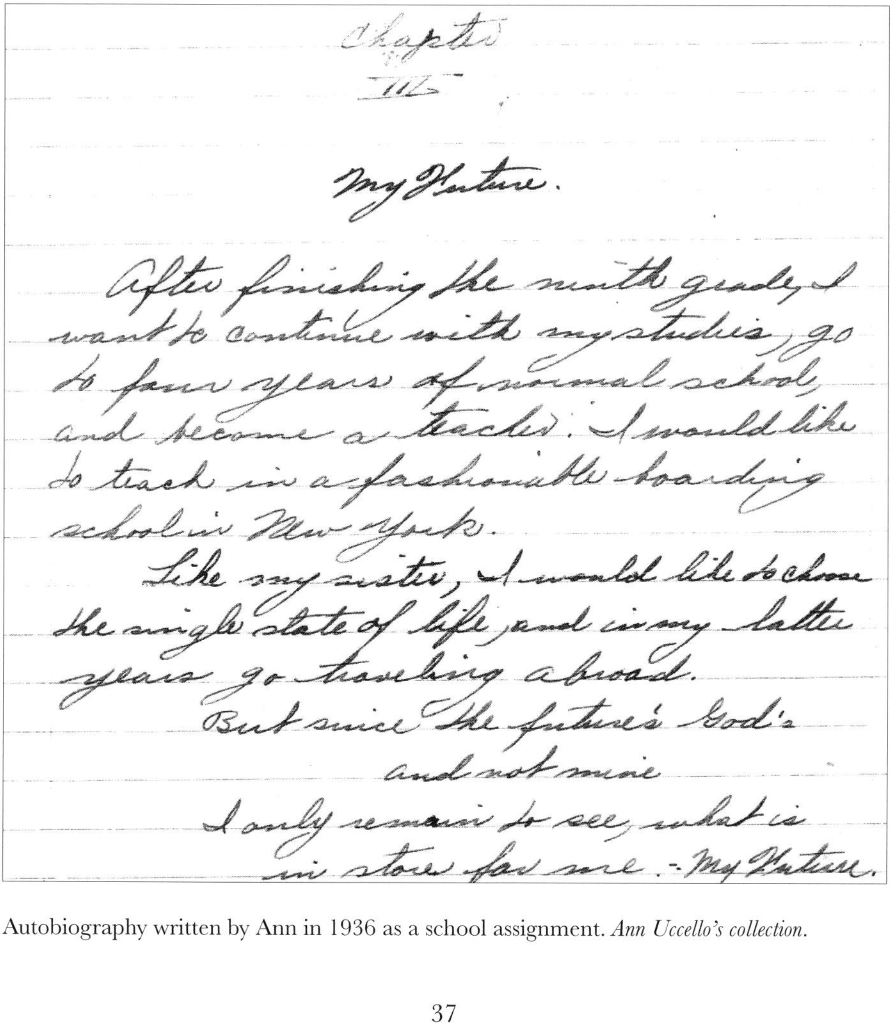
Chapter

III

My Future.

After finishing the ninth grade, I want to continue with my studies, go to four years of normal school, and become a teacher. I would like to teach in a fashionable boarding school in New York.

Like my sister, I would like to choose the single state of life and in my latter years go traveling abroad.

But since the future's God's
and not mine
I only remain to see, what is
in store for me. - My Future.

Autobiography written by Ann in 1936 as a school assignment. *Ann Uccello's collection.*

sister I would like to choose the single state of life, and in my latter years go traveling abroad. But since the future is God's and not mine, I only remain to see what is in store for me."

The influence of religion is also mentioned again in the same paper. She states, "I entered first grade at Holcomb St. School. In the middle of the year we moved, so I had to go to Northwest School. While I was in second grade, one of the greatest events in my life took place, I received the wonderful Sacrament of Holy Eucharist."

Most of Ann's friends were Jewish or Irish, but this did not mean that she was immune to the prejudices of the time, particularly so at Catholic school, where all the nuns were Irish and were not shy in singing the praises of their own. Even at commencement time from Saint Joseph College, Ann recalls, her very good friend, an Irish girl, told Ann that she could not attend the graduation party because she was Italian and they could not find an Irish boy for her. Ann did attend, on a double date with another girlfriend who had introduced Ann to an Italian boy.

But at times she would get the same treatment from Italian friends who would somehow resent that she had so many friends of Irish and Jewish descent. Perhaps as a result of these formative experiences, Ann does not have a racist bone in her body, and she has always treated one and all with the same degree of respect, no matter the social scale or the color of their skin or any other consideration.

The core of Ann's beliefs were formed during these times, and she would never deviate from them, no matter how convenient or politically correct it would have been to do so. She never used an obscene word and always told you what she thought. Honest, hardworking, thrifty, disciplined, serious, ambitious but not interested in money or power, strongly believing in social responsibility and socially progressive—that was and is Antonina "Ann" Uccello. The same qualities that so appealed to people who would elect her mayor of Hartford twice and almost send her to D.C. as a congresswoman were the same qualities that drove her opponents up a wall. They simply refused to believe that she would be interested in common sense solutions to the issues at hand and not interested in scoring political points. They refused to believe that she had no grand scheme, that she was not a "politician" in the sense that a politician would bend his or her beliefs to accommodate the needs to win an election.

A 1967 headline in the *Hartford Courant* read: "Uccello Denies She Is a Politician." The article went on to describe her as speaking her mind, saying she doesn't believe in making promises in exchange for votes and doesn't like the political games. She called herself a practical worker.

In a 1969 article in *Sign*, a Catholic publication, here is how she is described: "Ann is that paradox, the best of politician, the worst of politician: most of all, as noted by the Democrats, she confounds, she is just herself. As corny as it sounds her conscience is her guide."

In 1968, she told a Catholic high school audience that her slogan was "DPOCF"—Daily Practice of Catholic Faith. And how did she overcome her fears during the tense days of 1969 and the race riots? By carrying her secret weapon: her rosary beads.

In July 2014, I was sitting with Ann for lunch in the dining room of the complex where she lives. Next to us was a table with four people when a Jewish gentleman came by and recounted an old joke, only slightly off color. On his way out, he stopped to say hello to Ann and asked her if she had heard the joke and tried to repeat it, but Ann firmly stopped him. Her strong sense of values and faith would not allow her to listen to an off-color joke.

Chapter 3

The Education of Ann Uccello

The Antonina Uccello who graduated from Saint Joseph College with a BS in 1944 was an accomplished debater who was awarded honors in history and political science, a very religious person, still very much attached to her family, a voice to be reckoned with, ambitious and wanting to do good—but she was just not sure how.

In 1940, Ann had graduated from Weaver High School, which, back then, was predominantly Jewish with a few Italians and still fewer African Americans. She was a member of the French Club, and she counted Norman Lear, the famed TV producer, among her classmates.

She had wanted to go to Central Connecticut College, a teacher's school based in New Britain, and it made sense because Ann wanted to become a teacher, but she ended up at Saint Joseph College, an all-women college founded less than ten years earlier by the Sisters of Mercy as an adjunct to their widely known Mount St. Joseph Academy, a high school founded in 1854.

The college started out as a junior institution (a two-year program) with the dual objective of preparing students to continue their studies at four-year universities and, as outlined in the 1944 graduation program, "to

Opposite, top: Saint Joseph Junior High School, 1937 class graduation picture. *Ann Uccello's collection.*

Opposite, bottom: Ann was included in the list of the most prominent members of the 1940 class of Weaver High School. *Ann Uccello's collection.*

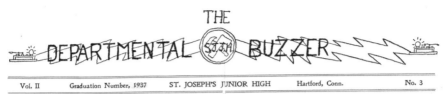

THE DEPARTMENTAL BUZZER

Vol. II | Graduation Number, 1937 | ST. JOSEPH'S JUNIOR HIGH | Hartford, Conn. | No. 3

WEAVER HIGH THE LOOKOUT

More Prominent Members in the Class '40

JULIUS FEGELMAN
Lookout Co-Business Manager

SHIRLEY WELSON
Speaker

Candidates For Graduation

Mr. Burke has released the following list of candidates for graduation:

Comeal Abbott, Nettie Mattie Abram, Marie Claire Adams, Leona Norma Alexander, Irene Martha Anderson, Shirley Mildred Anderson, Rita May Andreotta, Rosalyn Shirley Ascher, Marian Adele Bachrach, Miriam Rosalyn Baidack, Frances Alice Banton.

Josephine Loretta Baracchi, Claire Sonia Basch, Mary Agatha Beaudry, Eleanor Harriet Beckanstin, Selma Becker, Mary BenMaor, Jeanette Orise Benoit, Barbara Lucille Bernier, Estelle Mildred Blumberg, Myrtle Bobrow, Agnes Mary Brady, Rose Brenner, Dorothy Mae Brice, Betty Brody, Mae Pearl Brody, Enid Traub Brooks, Sylvia Brown.

Frances Priscilla Browne, Helen Ella Buckley, Vivian Louise Burgess, Gracie Mae Burney-Bey, Stella Calusine, Burt Norcross Cannon, Cecilia Anne Caputo, Ruby Carroll, Elizabeth Jean Case, Elizabeth Ann Celani, Dorothy Lillian Christensen, Marjorie Ruth Christensen, Dorothy Agnes Ciccone, Florence Lucille Cieri, Elaine Clark.

Frances Shirley Cohen, Ruth Roslyn Cohen, Beatrice Cohn, Bella Coiro, Ethel Beatrice Colton, Gloria Geraldine Composto, Helen Mary Conners, Janet Emily Cooley, Eileen Teresa Costello, Josephine Margaret Costello, Mary Theresa Cronin, Bernice Marie Curry, Elizabeth Ann D'Abato, Gertrude Josephine Dahl, Harriet Rose Danen, Elsie Alexander Dapko, Ida Sarah Darling.

Lillian Darling, Grace Gilmour Davidson, Rivel Jane Davidson, Sara Thelma Davidson, Lois Gertrude Davison, Anne Catherine DeFelice, Ann Katherine Delekta, Betty Charlena Devine, Yolanda Dorothy Diana, Catherine Elizabeth Dobruck, Elizabeth Joan Doocey, Annie Ruth Dowdell, Florence Drapel, Pauline Duval, Creola Janice Dwin, Anne Elson.

Ida Epstein, Kathryn Dion Faulkner, Virginia Ruth Faulkner, Sylvia Feldstein, Loretta Fiorinda Ferrigno, Florence Grace Fichman, Leona Fineberg, Anne Christie Flannagan, Mil-

ANTONINA UCCELLO
Speaker

PAUL BORSTEIN
Lookout Business Manager

ROSLYN PESSIN

RICHARD BYRNE

HARRY SMITH

EDITH WORTMAN

offer to others a finishing cultural education, while endowing them with such vocational power as shall enable them to become self sufficient and economically independent."

In 1932, the new college listed 65 day students and a faculty of fifteen. By 1942, the college had 250 students and a faculty of thirty-five. Promised average class size was 12.

Ann's sister Vincenza was strongly against Ann going to Saint Joseph. Her fear was that this Irish-Catholic school would discriminate against the Italian American student, a fear based on prior experience with similar schools. As fate would have it, Vincenza would become not only a graduate of the school but also its leading art professor, while sister Nellie and cousin Nellie would also graduate from Saint Joseph, as did four other cousins.

Money was also a consideration. The Uccello family simply could not afford the $200-per-year tuition. Discussions ensued between Ann's father and Sister Rosa, dean of Saint Joseph. Ann was admitted to the school while the parents agreed to a pay-as-you-go plan. Ann worked in the cafeteria to earn money to pay for school, and on Saturdays, she would work either at Brown Thompson or at a fashion store on Main Street across from G. Fox where she would sell hats and run the elevator. For the record, her parents paid to the last penny, and the benefits to Saint Joseph far exceed the "investment" the school made in Ann, who has made significant monetary and in-kind contributions to the growth of the school.

Ann and her parents on graduation day at Saint Joseph College, 1944. *Ann Uccello's collection.*

School was intense and demanding. Ann would have classes four days a week, with Wednesdays free for work on research and projects. She would walk to school from her home on Albany Avenue, down

Scarborough Street and up to the school on Asylum Avenue. Some days it was so cold that by the time she got to school, her fingers were frozen. Other times, a compassionate bus driver, with a bus only half full, would stop to offer a much-needed and welcome ride. Ann and her friends got together and bought the bus drivers a Christmas present.

Ann's graduation picture, 1944. *Ann Uccello's collection.*

Antonina was an excellent student and was extremely active in various clubs and societies. She was president of the French Club, vice-president of the Mendelian Club, secretary of the Debating Society and vice-president of the International Relations Club. She didn't participate in any sports activities, however. Her father considered sports unseemly for women.

In her four years at the institution, Ann formed some very special and long-lasting relationships that would influence her for the rest of her life. Sister Rosa and Professor Mary Holloran instilled in Ann the belief that she could aspire to and do anything she wanted and not to be limited by being a woman or an Italian American. When some work did not meet their expectations, they kept pushing her by telling her that she could do better. Sister Rosa gave Ann a B in philosophy and told her that she could do much better.

Sister Rosa left Saint Joseph College in 1950 to become head of the Sacred Heart Convent in Waterbury, and Professor Halloran left in August 1952 to join the Hampton Institute in Virginia. But Ann kept in touch with both for years thereafter, visiting Sister Rosa in Waterbury on many occasions and keeping up a frequent correspondence until her death in January 1961.

Sister Rosa was a strict disciplinarian. Ann remembers a dance where the girls were matched with the boys from the Holy Cross College and started to dance the "big apple"—a much milder form of the twist—only to be

Left: Sister Rosa, pictured in 1944. *Ann Uccello's collection.*

Below: Ann presents a going-away gift to Mary Halloran in 1952. At left is Governor Baldwin and, to his left, Senator Purtell. *Ann Uccello's collection.*

warned by Sister Rosa that they had crossed the line. The boys from Holy Cross were never again invited to Saint Joseph.

Monsignor Tuebings's philosophy class was one event each day that all students looked forward to and the reason why Vincenza and Nellie ended up going to Saint Joseph, for Ann would come home and recount his latest musings. Ann describes him as ahead of his time, a middle-aged, good-looking fatherly figure who had studied in France.

Ann's dating experience was sporadic, limited by her father and by herself. She recalls how she was supposed to go to one dance with a sailor stationed at Trinity College whom she had met at a meet and greet at Saint Joseph. She dressed up and went to the dance, but the sailor never showed up. Several days later, she received a very apologetic letter from him stating that he had some unexpected commitment, that he was very sorry and that his friends had told him that Ann looked beautiful. Ann recounts this while mimicking playing a violin.

One time, she was walking up Albany Avenue when a fellow standing at a street corner tried to get her attention but to no avail. She remembers that he yelled, "That's OK, I got wallpaper at home more stuck up than you."

Ann receiving her honorary doctorate from Saint Joseph College in 1971. *From left*: Senator Margaret Chase Smith, Ann, Nellie Uccello Romaine, Vincenza Uccello and their mother, Josephine. *Ann Uccello's collection.*

Ann loved school. She loved being busy and hated summers—"dullville," she defined them—broken by an occasional trip to the beach with Aunt Lucy, who was young enough to appreciate having the girls around for company. More often than not, they would pack a picnic and head to Keeney Park, with friends and relatives joining in.

Ann's work with the college began almost immediately after she graduated and would continue for the next seventy years. In 1949, she was instrumental in founding the Alumnae Office and became its executive secretary, work for which she was paid the grand total of $300 per year (that is correct—per *year*), but then again, she would work only one day a week. Now the department has a full-time director and several employees.

In 1971, Ann became the first alumna to receive an honorary doctorate in humane letters, and in 1978, she received the Distinguished Alumna Award.

Chapter 4

The Early Years

1944–63

Twenty-two years old and looking much younger, Ann entered the workforce shortly after graduation from Saint Joseph College in June 1944. She accepted a position as a high school teacher in the town of East Hampton, which would turn out to be both the beginning and the end of the teaching career she had so aspired to from an early age.

Everything about the job turned out to be much more challenging than Ann ever imagined. Just getting to East Hampton was not easy and required Ann to take a bus from the Blue Hills Avenue apartment she lived in with her parents and sisters to Central Row in downtown Hartford; from there, she traveled to Middletown and from Middletown to East Hampton. She would leave for the job on Sunday afternoon and return home to her parents and sisters on Friday night.

And for the first time, she would not be living at home. In East Hampton, she lived with a very nice and proper English family, but it was not exactly the bubbly lifestyle she was used to.

The teaching part of the job was also extremely challenging—as challenging as any first-year teaching job could be and more. Ann was twenty-two and looked even younger than some of her students. Some of the boys would playfully flirt with her.

A disciplinarian with a strict sense of duty, she found her style challenged in many ways, which, in retrospect, contributed in no small part to her decision not to return to East Hampton.

East Hampton High School graduating class of 1945, with Ann seated at bottom right. Future Connecticut governor Bill O'Neil was a member of this class. *Ann Uccello's collection.*

The 1985 fortieth class reunion of 1945 East Hampton High graduates with now Governor O'Neil. *Ann Uccello's collection.*

Her experience there was not a positive one, but it did produce one significant benefit: Bill O'Neil was one of Ann's students and would become governor following the death of Ella Grasso and then be reelected on his own merit. The governor never forgot the contribution Ann made to his life, and during his tenure, he showed as much with many kind gestures.

In the summer of 1945, an unemployed Ann went job searching again. She was offered a position at Aetna in the legal department (in those days, she had decided that to succeed in politics you had to be a lawyer and had taken some law courses), but she eventually decided to accept a position at G. Fox and Co., the famed department store in downtown Hartford, which for decades was the choice destination for shoppers from Hartford and surrounding towns. Ann would remain there until 1967, when she took a leave of absence following her election as mayor of Hartford, and would leave permanently in 1969, when she won reelection.

The position at G. Fox was interesting, challenging and gave her the opportunity to be noticed by Mrs. Auerbach, the owner. Ann managed a cadre of employees who would keep track of all items sold at the store so that they could provide timely information to the buyers heading to New York on what was selling, and over time, she would also become responsible for some financial functions. But most important of all, in 1960, she was asked to become Mrs. Auerbach's assistant after a previous employee who had been at the owner's side for years left under not totally clear circumstances. Ann was efficient, disciplined and trustworthy—everything the owner appreciated in a position as sensitive as this one.

Only once does Ann recall not following the wishes of her boss. An incident had taken place at the store in which one of the employees had committed an infraction, but Ann decided to deal with him directly by giving the fellow a warning. Mrs. Auerbach wanted to know all of the details, but Ann simply informed her that she had dealt with it and no further action was needed. It was the one and only time that the owner reminded Ann of who was in charge. The next day, she called Ann into her office and told her that she had handled the matter correctly, but Ann never disclosed the identity of the individual.

And, of course, the widely reported story is that Ann, before accepting a position on the ticket of the New GOP, asked for Mrs. Auerbach's blessing. She had been traveling and, upon returning that evening, was asked and gave an enthusiastic approval to the budding political career of Antonina "Ann" Uccello. Not Mrs. Auerbach and not even Ann could have possibly imagined in their wildest dreams the importance of that first step and the significant impact Ann would have on Hartford, the state and the country.

Outside of work, Ann was focused on her political and social activities. She had registered as a Republican upon turning twenty-one, and she had begun to attend meetings and would volunteer for the routine tasks of campaigns (mailing postcards, hanging signs, etc.). She was an active member of the Young GOP Organization, of which she became recording secretary in 1956, and she was co-chair of a dance for Young GOP members and chairman of the annual Young GOP picnic.

In 1960, she played an active role in the Nixon campaign in Connecticut. She was chosen to be a sergeant-at-arms at the July convention in Chicago that nominated Nixon. She played an active role in reaching out on behalf of the GOP volunteers for Nixon's organization and was appointed chairman of the local Nixon for President Club.

In July 1960, she traveled to Chicago to attend the convention. She was gone only for a few days, but her mother and sister still sent her a letter updating her on family life—that is how close this family was. I have reproduced a copy of the letter in one of the following pages. Her mother's English was not the queen's English, but the love is genuine.

Ann was active in the Young Italian American Ladies Auxiliary (she helped file the papers with the secretary of state to incorporate the organization) and was also very active at her alma mater, Saint Joseph College. On several occasions, she was asked to chair an organization but never accepted, wishing instead to be able to keep her options open.

The Catholic Graduates Club of Greater Hartford was the major focus of Ann's social activities. In 1961, she was the chair of the event committee of the Catholic Graduates Club, and in that capacity, she was responsible for the Gala Scolaire, a black-tie concert organized to celebrate the tenth anniversary of the founding of the Catholic Graduate Club and to raise funds for a scholarship.

Her attention to details and organizing skills were on full display. She issued a two-page memo dated May 25, 1960, addressed to the executive committee of the club in which she outlined the objectives of the event, the cost, the location, the invitations and every other detail one can possibly imagine. She even wrote to the pope requesting a special message. She received a letter from the Vatican secretary of state, informing Ann that they do not issue such requests as they are too many but assuring her that His Holiness would pray for the success of her event.

Without full awareness of it at the time, she was building the kind of network that would be so useful in her political career. But the many years

Ann chaired the annual ball celebrating the tenth anniversary of the Catholic Graduate Club in 1961. *Ann Uccello's collection.*

between graduation in 1944 and her first run for political office in 1963 were also filled with family events that helped shape her life.

In 1950, Vincenza and Ann took a month-long vacation to Europe (they traveled aboard the legendary *Queen Elizabeth*), which included a one-week stay in Canicattini Bagni, the birthplace of her parents. Here she visited her paternal grandmother, whom she had so adored and had not seen since 1928. It was an opportunity to visit Siracusa and the impressive archaeological

Ann and her paternal grandmother in Canicattini in 1950. *Ann Uccello's collection.*

remains of the first Greek colony outside Greece and the home of the famed mathematician Archimedes. This visit reinforced the bond that Ann and the entire family felt to this tiny village in southeast Sicily that had been so important to her parents and in which she had lived for almost eighteen months. The sisters, who could speak fluent Sicilian, were very much at home in this environment.

In 1951, she wrote a report on the trip in the winter issue of the *Bulletin* published by the Alumnae Association of Saint Joseph College. The article is a window into Ann's values. She recounts the visit to Rome and the special privilege of not only seeing Pope Pius XII at Saint Peter but also attending a semiprivate audience (eighty-two people total) with the pope at Castel Gandolfo, the summer residence of the pope fifteen miles away from Rome. A strict dress code required some last-minute creativity to make sure they were properly dressed (they had not known about the semiprivate visit until a day earlier). They waited anxiously as the pope made his way through the line of guests, and when their turn arrived, Ann asked Pope Pius if he remembered his visit to Saint Joseph College. His eyes sparkled, and he said, "Ah, yes. Then a special blessing for the college." To Ann, that was by far the highlight of her trip abroad and an

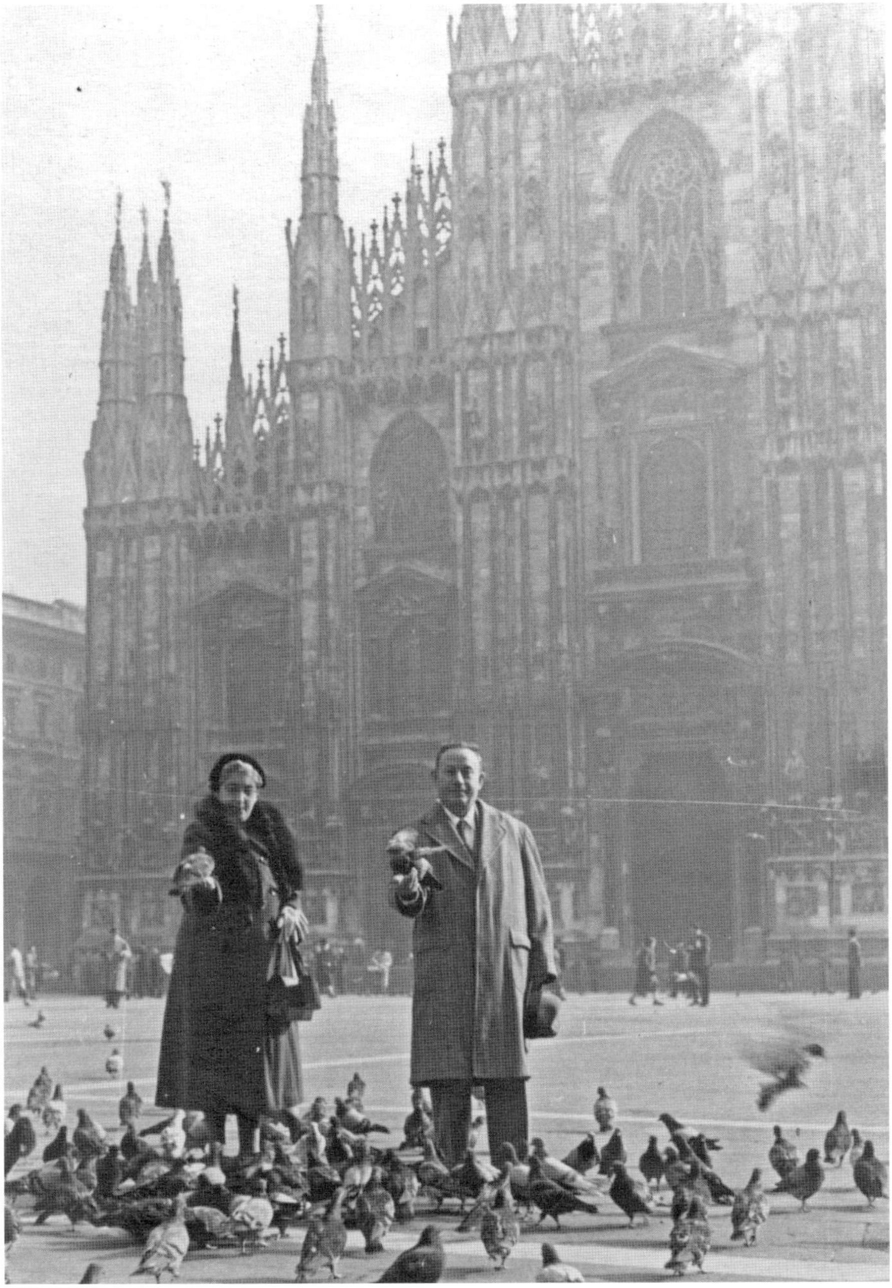

Mr. and Mrs. Uccello in Milan, Italy, on their way to a visit to Canicattini in 1954. *Ann Uccello's collection.*

This 1954 photograph shows Mr. and Mrs. Uccello in front of the house he was born in. *Ann Uccello's collection.*

experience that further strengthened the faith she had so nurtured from a very young age.

In 1954, it was her parents' turn to visit Italy as a celebration of Salvatore's retirement. Ann borrowed $1,000 to help pay for the trip and was somewhat shocked when the borrowing request turned out to be much easier than expected. Somehow she had envisioned dozens of questions and documents, but the loan officer at the local bank simply asked a few questions and came back with a check for $1,000.

This trip was the only diversion from everyday life the Uccellos had experienced since their wedding. No yearly vacations (no money) and no weekend trips (no car) meant that attendance at the opera at the Bushnell was the only extravagance the family could afford.

Salvatore and Josephine returned "home" to their families in Canicattini, the only such trip the couple would make together back to their roots. But they also

Mr. and Mrs. Uccello on the occasion of the marriage of their daughter Carmela in 1952. *Ann Uccello's collection.*

Mr. and Mrs. Uccello, proud grandparents of a male child, David, in 1956. *Ann Uccello's collection.*

had an opportunity to travel to Italy, and their picture at Piazza Duomo in Milan shows a happy couple enjoying a little bit of the good life, a life that for them had previously been focused on work and home.

Life at home on Blue Hills Avenue was changing in many ways. In 1952, Carmela married Russell Gustafson, and they would go on to have two children, a boy and a girl. When told of the birth of his first grandchild—a boy—in 1956, Ann's father remarked, "Are you sure?" I guess after five daughters he could not believe that finally the family had produced a male. A picture of Salvatore holding the baby shows as wide a smile on Salvatore's face as anyone had ever seen before.

Ann's father retired in 1954, and the family moved to Branford Street. Vincenza had returned to school and was attending Saint Joseph College, graduating in 1956, the first of what would turn out to be a lifetime of graduations for this perpetual student.

Gil had graduated from the Central Connecticut Teacher College, while Nellie had followed in the footsteps of Ann and Vincenza and graduated from Saint Joseph College, where she became school paper editor. She took a teaching position in South Windsor and here would meet fellow teacher Steve Romaine, whom she married in 1962. Gil married Al Martini in 1968.

Chapter 5

Hartford Town Council

1963–67

Ann Uccello burst into the political scene in the election of 1963. An unknown quantity to most voters and to her own party, she would become mayor just a short four years later and would barely miss being elected congresswoman in 1970.

People underestimated Ann from the very beginning and did not perceive the many qualities that the voters so admired and that allowed her, a Republican, to win election after election in a heavily Democratic city.

Critics belittled her claim that she was not a politician, but she was not. Opponents underestimated how determined a foe she could be and deceived themselves by focusing on her youthful appearance. People underestimated the strength of the family values she brought to her campaign, just as she had brought to any of her undertakings, whether at work or in one of the many social causes and clubs to which she devoted her time. And people perhaps conveniently forgot that Ann was a champion debater while at Saint Joseph.

Sister Rosa, the dean at Saint Joseph College, had told her over and over again that she could do anything she wanted to. And Ann had learned a lot from Mrs. Auerbach, the G. Fox owner and Ann's boss for several years, a determined, petite woman who knew what she wanted to do and was not shy in expressing her opinion.

"Dear, one day you will be mayor of Hartford," said Mrs. Auerbach once to a stunned Ann on one of only two or three occasions that they ever spoke of politics. And her words would prove to be prophetic. The only other political advice from Mrs. Auerbach came following Ann's election on the Court of

Common Council. "Now, dear, you two [Ann and Betty Knox] act like ladies." The two were not close but were not enemies either. Ann came from the immigrant family, while Betty walked the same social circles as Mrs. Auerbach.

In a way, Mrs. Auerbach had seen qualities in Ann that not even Ann had perhaps yet fully detected. She had never aspired to become mayor, as she did not have specific political aspirations. But once in the arena, she would apply herself to the fullest extent of her ability. Opponents would see a "grand plan" and would charge that her demeanor was a farce, that she was as political as or more so than any other. But they were dead wrong on all those counts.

Ann possesses intangible assets that all politicians would love to have: she is likeable, personable and trustworthy. She stands for values, and she would not compromise those for any political office.

Critics misconstrued this self-assurance and this belief in her values and criticized her "holier than thou" attitude. But she was not an uncompromising lightning rod, as some of today's politicians pretend to be to obtain notoriety.

Ann is the first one to give credit for the political success to her campaign manager, George Ducharme (the General, as he was known), and to Mary Barry, both colleagues at G. Fox and also both members of the Graduate Catholic Club. George and Mary applied themselves on Ann's behalf with a vigor and dedication unmatched by anyone else except Ann herself and Ann's mother. They believed in Ann's potential and capabilities and proved to have the type of organizational skills that made the difference in Ann's campaign. Before Ann ever ran for office, she had to get on a GOP ticket that was pretty much all set. Mary and George collected the necessary signatures to make sure that she was on the ballot.

But the circle of volunteers was much larger and, of course, included all her sisters and, oh yes, the "Admiral," as Ann's mother was known around the political circle. She would cook for the volunteers, but she was very involved in the campaign herself. Her relatives had served as mayor of the small city of her birth, and some of the old DNA must have been transmitted to Josephine and then to Ann.

On the other hand, Ann's father was largely absent from the political hoopla. He never discouraged Ann but never encouraged her either, probably fearing that she might get hurt. In the last few years of her career, he was in ill health and unable to fully comprehend or participate in all that was happening.

But let's go back to the beginning. Ann was a registered Republican since age twenty-one, having been active in party politics with the Young

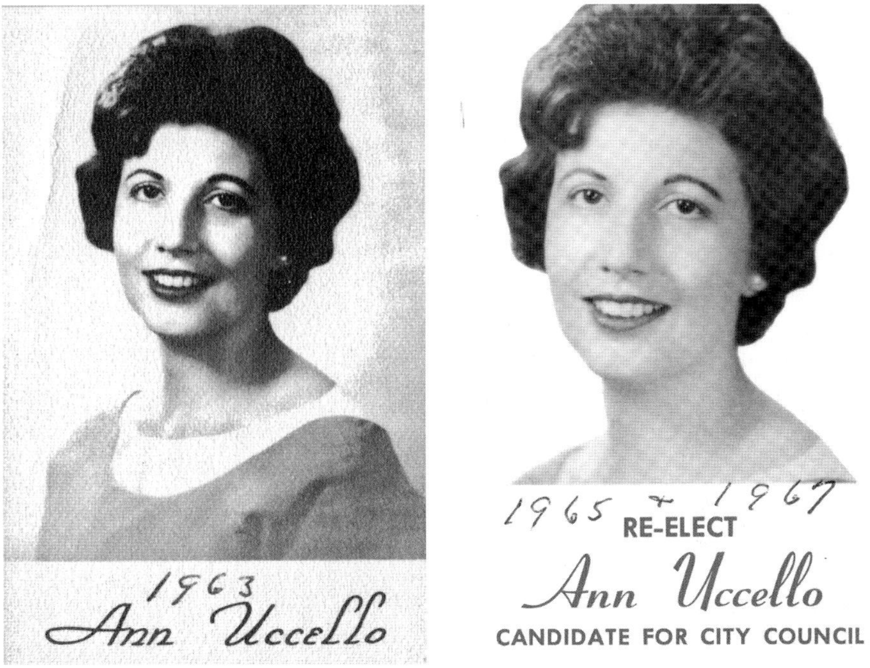

Campaign literature for town council. *Ann Uccello's collection.*

Republicans association. She did all the tedious but necessary work needed to get out the vote and win elections.

The problem was that in the 1950s and early '60s, the GOP in Hartford was a nonentity. City chairman Pat De Pasquale (of the famous De Pasquale Restaurant on Front Street, a legendary place on the Italian East Side) was an amiable but ineffective leader. The last GOP mayor had been elected in 1945, and since that time, the Republicans had fielded a slate only once, and no one from that slate had been elected.

The City of Hartford election system consisted of a "non-partisan" slate of eighteen people who were endorsed by the Citizens Charter Committee and would run in an October primary to whittle the number down to twelve. This was followed by the election in November, with the top nine elected. Just before the 1963 election, the Democrats controlled the city Court of Common Council by eight to one.

The failure of Chairman De Pasquale to be able to field a GOP slate for the '63 election was the proverbial straw that broke the camel's back. Led by Howard Kaufman, deputy registrar of voters in Hartford, and with the help of Bill Marsh, chairman of the Citizens Committee, they put together a slate that, in addition to Marsh, included attorney Ted Di Lorenzo and Al Miller, a broker. They called themselves the "New Republican Party."

Ann Uccello was not part of the Court of Common Council slate announcement and was instead asked to run for the board of education, which she refused to do. At a meeting of the new group, Ann, a member of the town Republican committee, was asked to wait outside while the others discussed her future. She was opposed by Attorney Rittenband on the ground that the group would lose credibility by adding her to the Court of Common Council list after already having issued the names of their candidates. Fortunately, the majority sided with Ann. Rittenband went on to become one of Ann's strongest supporters, and when she became mayor, he also would "serve" her informally as the GOP corporation counsel and senior policy advisor and would work with Ann to write most of the speeches she gave.

Formation of the new group took place over the Labor Day weekend, and the deadline for new candidates was that Wednesday. They each needed 250 signatures to be placed on the ballot, which they accomplished just before the 4:30 deadline on Wednesday. The New GOP group also created an awkward situation with GOP incumbent Betty Knox, an institution within the GOP and the only sure vote getter among Republicans. Knox had fielded her own GOP slate.

The primary election was a big eye-opener, as the new GOP slate would place three of its four candidates in the field of twelve finalists from whom the city Court of Common Council members would be chosen. Ann finished first among the four with over 4,500 votes—just a small taste of things to come. In the general election of 1963, Ann finished in an amazing seventh place, running ahead of Betty Knox and Di Lorenzo, who also were elected to the city Court of Common Council.

For the new GOP, this was a major victory. It had placed two of its candidates on the Court of Common Council and had sliced the Democrats' margin from eight to one to six to three. The GOP would not be in control of the council, but it had made a statement that it would be a force nonetheless.

This election established Ann as the fresh face of the Hartford GOP. It also marked the beginning of a collaboration with two key advisors: George Ducharme, campaign manager, and Richard Rittenband, legal and policy advisor.

George Ducharme may have been the second-most important man in Ann's life; her father, of course, was the first. Ducharme became a member of the family, the brother that the sisters never had. George and his tremendous

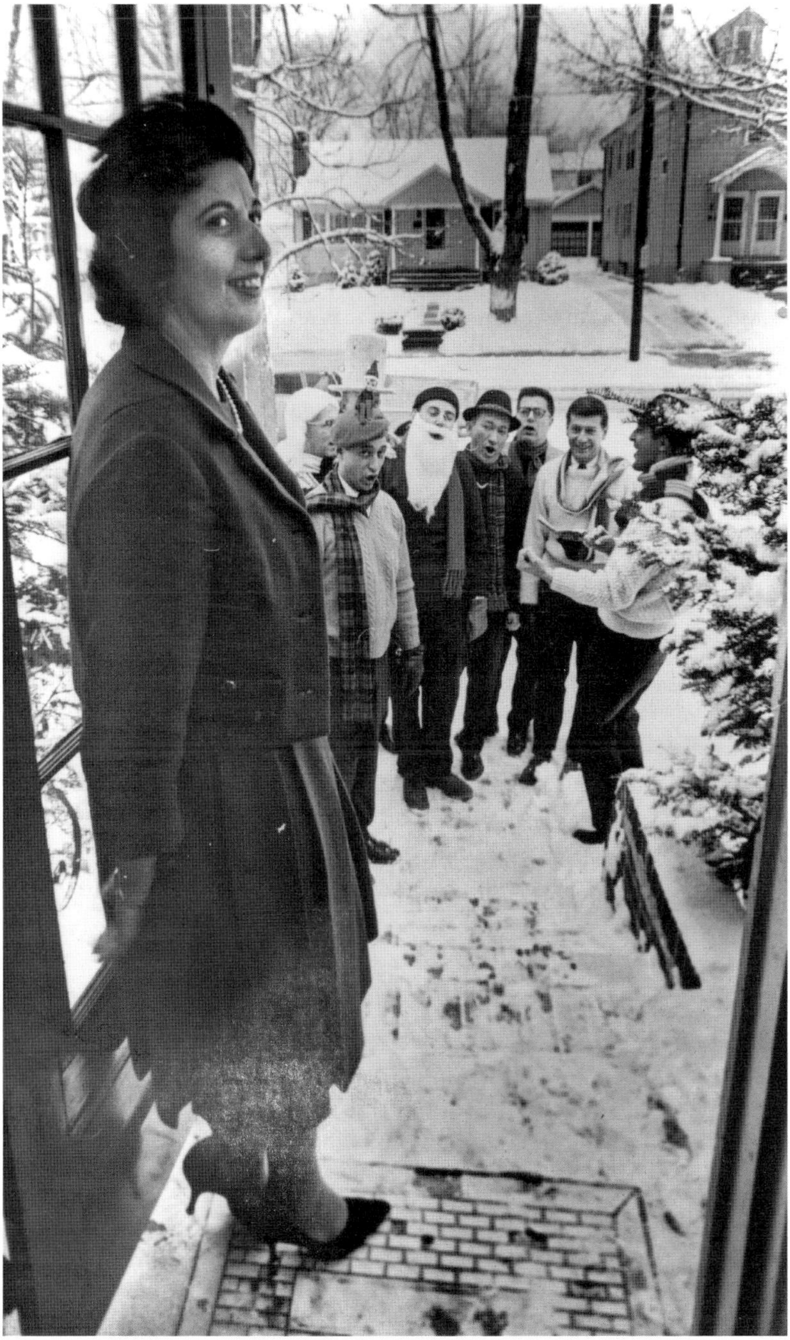

Christmas carols by the Cape Apes, friends of Ann who would vacation at Cape Cod, in 1964. *Ann Uccello's collection.*

marketing and organizing skills made it possible for Ann to break through in the political world. He was a colleague at G. Fox, and it was Ann who introduced him to the activities of the Catholic Graduates Club. Occasionally, he would accompany Ann to social events, as he was also single.

He first got involved in Ann's campaign because he felt she would lose badly and her feelings would be hurt. But to his credit, he recognized early on the intangible qualities that would make Ann the formidable candidate she would become. And it was George who, in 1965, told Ann that she would be elected mayor. I don't believe Ann had any such aspirations or had even thought that far into her political future.

In 1965, George did the unthinkable: he quit a senior paid position at G. Fox to run Ann's campaign. He would not get another full-time job until 1971, following Ann's defeat in the congressional election.

He never asked for and was never given anything in return. No wonder the speculation about their relationship was rampant. Who does something for nothing? They must have slept together, or he must have been independently wealthy, according to the rumors. But if you believe in God, and they both do, maybe, just maybe, he was God's instrument, the guiding force that looks over us and gets us to a destination.

George was the friend who saw Ann's potential and helped her realize that potential with hard work and perseverance. In a way, George and Ann have a lot in common, as they do what they believe in without first analyzing all of the political consequences or how it would benefit or hurt them.

For someone who had never before been involved in politics, George was a fast learner. He would attend Court of Common Council meetings and sit in a corner next to a different group of attendees each time so that he could overhear their conversations about the council members and Ann in particular. He used the feedback to make sure they were on the right path.

He was also an innovative marketing manager, not afraid to speak his mind and challenge the status quo, which invariably meant that he would run afoul of the GOP establishment. He built, with the help of Mary Barry, a formidable ground operation that was the envy of the Democrats.

You would think that the campaign manager of a novice candidate who manages to finish seventh in her first election and fourth in the second would be sought after for his acumen. But instead of going after him to help the GOP run its campaign, George was largely ignored by Howard Hausman, GOP state chair.

George had come up with a very effective way of making sure that voters did not throw away Ann's campaign literature. Each election, he produced

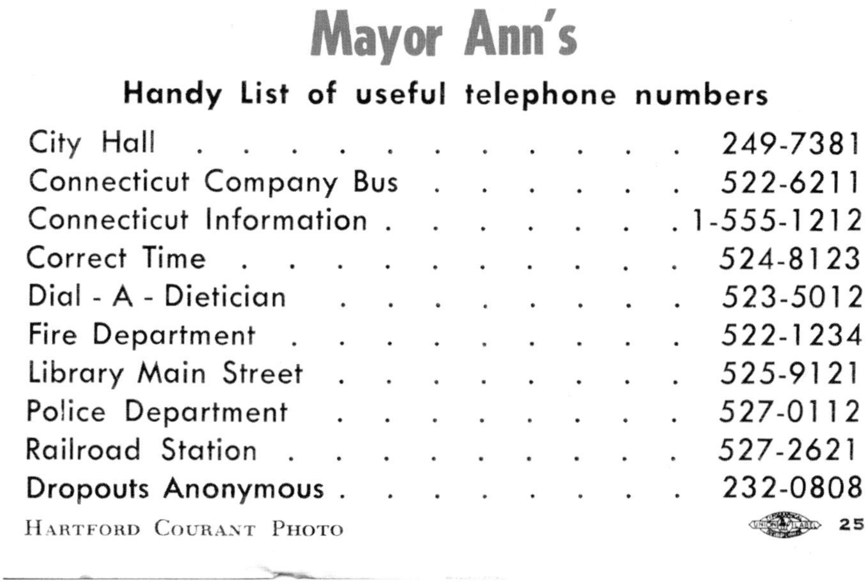

Mayor Ann's

Handy List of useful telephone numbers

City Hall	249-7381
Connecticut Company Bus	522-6211
Connecticut Information	1-555-1212
Correct Time	524-8123
Dial - A - Dietician	523-5012
Fire Department	522-1234
Library Main Street	525-9121
Police Department	527-0112
Railroad Station	527-2621
Dropouts Anonymous	232-0808

HARTFORD COURANT PHOTO 25

The 1969 campaign literature with some useful numbers. Voters would almost never throw them away. *Ann Uccello's collection.*

a small business card featuring Ann on the front and some useful phone numbers on the back. He figured that the people would keep them in their wallets as an easy reference point for those phone numbers, and he was right. In 1967 and '69, people would take out the old cards from their wallets and replace them with the new ones.

George was an outstanding asset—and at times a liability. Outspoken and brash, he did not always endear himself to the powers that be, but he did what he felt was best for Ann.

Rittenband, on the other hand, married and an attorney who would go on to become a judge, at first opposed including Ann on the New GOP ticket. The press had already been given the names of their slate, and he did not want to make a change that would show them to be inefficient or inept. Fortunately, he was overruled, and after that first conflict, he became Ann's political and legal advisor.

Rittenband and Ducharme had their differences, with one being more cautious and policy focused while the other was more brash and innovative, but both served Ann extremely well and loyally.

When Ann's work on the council and as mayor required a legal opinion, she got an informal one from Rittenband and not just from the corporation counsel, whom she felt would give a "Democrat" opinion. And he would be present in 1970 at various meetings with Weicker when Ann was deciding what elected position she would run for out of U.S. representative, U.S. senator and governor. He also became a consultant to Ann when she took over as director of consumer affairs at DOT in Washington and would accompany her on some of the public hearings she conducted across the country. In 1972, Rittenband was the GOP nominee for the First Congressional District but lost to Cotter.

Ann was always very mindful that, as a single woman, rumors were bound to fly about her close association with George Ducharme, and she did her best to maintain a distance and a proper relationship at all times. But she also felt a little guilt toward Dick Rittenband's wife because she would spend so much time together with him.

Ann recalled one "embarrassing" moment. It must have been about 2:00 a.m. when Ann and Councilman Bennet, an African American, were leaving the Sonesta Hotel after a lengthy budget meeting. The two had stepped outside to get into the back of a police cruiser that would take them home. At the same time, in walked a distinguished couple, sharply dressed, going back to their hotel room. Ann blushed at what the strangers must have thought of seeing a black man and a white woman going into the back of a police cruiser.

In a way, the election to the council was more exciting than the work on the council. Ann describes her first two years as "speaking in the wind"—she made general statements but had no control over any one issue. However, she did establish a very good working relationship with Mayor William E. Glynn and made substantive contributions to the council discussions. People knew she was not just a pretty face—she was a person to be reckoned with, not shy about expressing her opinion and someone who did her homework.

"But the New Republicans are equally aware of their responsibility to Hartford Citizens. Thus they are armed with ideas about education, housing, health, taxes, and, significantly, about responsiveness of Council members to their constituents." So wrote John Lacy in the *Hartford Courant* on December 1, 1963, just a few days before the new members would be sworn in on the council. This last issue of responsiveness was one of the arching themes of the '63 campaign: the New GOP was accusing the Democrats of being ruled by one man, John Bailey, who would control the names of those selected to run on the Democratic slate.

John Bailey was indeed such a force. As the state party chair, he was also chair of the National Democratic Party and a legendary political figure in the Hartford scene for decades.

Ann recalled one exchange she had with Bailey after her victory as mayor in 1967. He told her that if he had wanted to, he could have defeated her. She took it as a comment made in frustration by someone not used to losing. The fact is that many Democrats—and, of course, especially the Italians in Hartford—simply loved and respected Ann and broke rank with party leaders to give her some resounding personal victories.

Ann was appointed chair of the Human Resources Committee, and she used this position to show her metal and initiative. In 1964, all city employees were pegged to the same pay scale, but blue-collar workers had the support of the Democrats to increase their salary ranges without a corresponding increase for the police force. Deputy Mayor George B. Kinsella was in favor of such a move, but Mayor Glynn was not. The issue came up at a Court of Common Council meeting while Mayor Glynn was in Washington, D.C., and the Democrats rammed through the resolution against the united opposition of the GOP.

Council members would soon learn about Ann's resiliency and creativity. She introduced a separate resolution whereby the police officers' pay scale would be tied to that of the blue-collar workers, and the Democrats could not help but go along with it. She had outwitted the Democrats, prompting one of the members to say, "We knew you were pretty, but we did not realize you also have a brain." And she had earned the everlasting gratitude and support of the police force.

Such victories were clearly the exception. "GOP Councilmen Find Jobs Frustrating!" So screamed the headline on page 3b of the *Hartford Courant* in November 1964. "Councilmen Di Lorenzo and Uccello have proven themselves to be capable city legislators. Miss Uccello in particular is held in high non partisan esteem." But esteem did not mean that her ideas were accepted or that the GOP would gain access to patronage jobs. After a vote that placed only Democrats on the tax review board, Ann said to a fellow councilman, "Couldn't you give us at least one seat on the tax board?" To which the Democratic councilman replied, with a smile, "Ann, you didn't have the votes." On another occasion, she was told that "justice and fairness had nothing to do with politics."

By exercising total control over the city council proceedings and appointments, the Democrats were unknowingly giving Ann and the GOP the arching theme on which they would base their campaign: one of fairness and of minority representation on the council and railing against the one-party rule and, for that matter, the one-man rule imposed by John Bailey.

Ann did find some creative ways to make her points with the majority. Council Democrats were notorious for not showing up on time for the start of the council meetings, leaving the GOP (and Mayor Glynn) waiting and fuming. One such evening at 8:45 p.m., the Democrats had still not shown, and the majority of council members present, led by Ann and Betty Knox, had enough and introduced a resolution adjourning the meeting. Corporation counsel ruled that the GOP members were within their right to do so. "I think she got us" was the reply by the corporation counsel. "We are not here to play games," thundered a frustrated Ann.

Embarrassed, Democrats had learned once again at their own expense that they may have had a majority, but the opposition was alert and vibrant.

In 1965, Democrats handed Ann another opportunity to score points while enhancing her political stature. It started with a resolution that Ann presented in the form of a poem to refurbish the fountains outside city hall, which were not working: "Whereas the spring has sprung and the grass has riz, and whereas in front of City Hall two dry fountains thereis and whereas at the Capital Plaza and square we see beautiful fountains shooting the breeze 'tis sad to see the City Hall fountain die."

The Democrats took the opportunity to needle Ann on how a conservative could possibly propose and support such expenditures, as it would be a waste of taxpayers' money. Undaunted, Ann turned the table once again on them by announcing that she would organize a Fountain Ball to raise money for the project. She informed council Democrats that she was going to place their wives on the committee and that they would be forced to attend and support the event.

And so it was. The *Hartford Courant* and the *Harford Times* reported heavily about the ball in their society pages, such as the article in September 1965 featuring the slate of women making up the committee: Ms. Uccello, Mrs. Glynn, Mrs. Kinsella and Mrs. Ritter. "It's a ball in the fall at City Hall," started the article in one newspaper recounting how the event came to be.

For the next three years, the Fountain Ball held at city hall was the highlight of the social season, attended by political and business leaders, Democrats and Republicans. The fountains started to flow once again and continue to do so.

Ann's schedule was taxing, to say the least. She continued to work at G. Fox (her council position did not earn a salary, and the family needed the money), and she continued to participate in the many social activities and especially the Catholic organizations that had been at the core of her life

The 1965 cover of the program guide for the first Fountain Ball, designed by Ann's sister Vincenza. *Ann Uccello's collection.*

prior to the run for city council. The city council meetings often ran into the early hours, the outreach work of the New GOP had to continue and Ann was in high demand for appearances at social and civic events.

In 1965, the city hall atrium was turned into the main dance floor. *Ann Uccello's collection.*

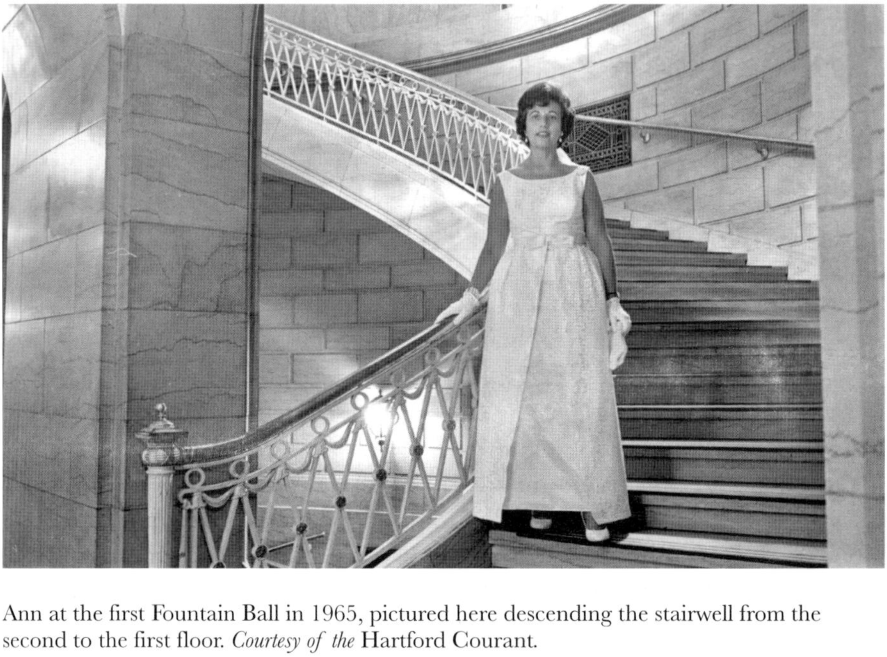

Ann at the first Fountain Ball in 1965, pictured here descending the stairwell from the second to the first floor. *Courtesy of the* Hartford Courant.

The 1965 Fountain Ball. Mr. and Mrs. Kinsella at left; George Ducharme and Ann Uccello at right. *Courtesy of the* Hartford Courant.

In August 1965, Ann announced that she and Councilman Di Lorenzo would be running for reelection. In their announcements, they touted their accomplishments, including more lights in city streets (Ann had first raised this issue during the 1963 campaign, and as unimportant as it may appear, it was exactly the kind of issue that resonated with voters), and they vowed to continue to be "constructive, effective independent and unbossed on the city council." John Bailey was never too far from their minds.

The 1965 election witnessed a number of developments that would enhance Ann's stature and allow her to become mayor just two short years later. Mayor Glynn, a conservative Democrat, chose not to run for a third term. He had never been a favorite of the party leadership, but the Democrats underestimated the difficulty this move would generate. Councilmen George B. Kinsella (the heir to a Hartford political dynasty that had already produced two prior mayors) and George J. Ritter began an intense rivalry.

The election results of November 1965 produced a number of surprises: Kinsella won the most votes, thus becoming mayor, while Ritter came in second and thus would be deputy mayor. Ann Uccello ran fourth (at first she was reported in fifth place, but a recount showed her in fourth), and the Democratic control of the city council was reduced from six to three to five to four. Elected in 1965 with the GOP slate was Colin Bennet, an African American.

The New GOP was elated with the results. It showed that the party's message resonated with the voters, who were more than willing to cross party lines to elect capable and competent candidates, no matter where they came from.

The bitterness between Kinsella and Ritter did not stop with the election, and three Democratic council members (Ritter, Corrigan and DeLucco) formed an alliance with the four Republicans (Uccello, Di Lorenzo, Ladd and Bennet) and established a working majority that would effectively control city hall for the next two years and which relegated Mayor Kinsella and his lone ally, Councilman Kelly, to figureheads.

In February 1966, an irate Mayor Kinsella and Councilman Kelly showed up at a Saturday budget meeting scheduled without the mayor to complain about not being involved in the process. And, in fact, the working majority had met in a hotel room the night before, ironed out all their differences and were presenting Mayor Kinsella with a fait accompli. It would not be the last time.

In March 1966, Councilman Bennet proposed a resolution transferring the appointment powers to city commissions from the mayor to the Court of Common Council, and that same month, the council voted to appoint Councilman Corrigan and not Mayor Kinsella to the nascent Regional Council of Elected Officials. "Open Season on Mayor Continues," screamed the headline in the March 20, 1966 edition of the *Hartford Courant*.

The issue of cooperating with the three Democrats, however, was not without risk to the image of the four GOP council members who, until then, had run on being the independent voice of Hartford voters. "The

Republican Councilmen have melted into a faceless coalition," wrote James O'Hara, then the *Courant* political reporter.

Ann continued to work hard and on at least one occasion showed her independence by voting against the coalition of which she was a part. She continued to attend social events, to be a voice of common reason within the council and to earn the admiration of voters.

In June 1966, the animosity between Kinsella and Ritter worked very much in her favor when she was asked by Kinsella to represent the City of Hartford at the U.S. Conference of Mayors in Dallas. In a press release, Mayor Kinsella noted, "Miss Uccello will bring the conference fresh ideas and realistic approaches." And while that was indeed true, it was also true that not appointing Ritter to the position would be a personal slight.

Ella Grasso, then secretary of state, was one politician who was not happy with Kinsella appointing Uccello to the Conference of Mayors. She apparently called the mayor to complain about how he could possibly present such an opportunity to the opposition and perhaps future political rival.

Ella, who would go on to become governor, and Ann had a lot in common and yet had many significant differences. Both were Italian Americans, both very intelligent and ambitious, but where Ella was a John Bailey Democrat, Ann was more of a freelancer who never really became a party favorite.

In 1970, Ann had wanted to run for governor, and if the polls of the day were correct, she would have had a very good chance of winning that election. Of course, she ran for Congress and lost, while a few years later, Ella would run for governor and win.

The dawn of 1967 opened with the political pundits continuing to focus on the personal battle between Kinsella and Ritter and speculating on how this would all work out in the upcoming election. Some people pointed out that this could be the year for Ann Uccello to shoot at the number one position. She had been the top Republican vote-getter the last time around, and it would be logical that she would become the standard-bearer for the GOP in the extremely unlikely chance of an election victory.

In early 1967, the GOP council members had started to focus their attention on the Hartford taxpayers and what they considered their unfairly high rate. In a letter to Governor Dempsey in February 1967, the four complained that the property tax burden in Hartford had reached "its saturation point" and was driving people away from the city. Nothing of significance came from the initiative, and almost fifty years later, their fears have been unfortunately fulfilled: Hartford has become a predominantly minority city, a process that has exacerbated the financial difficulties of the

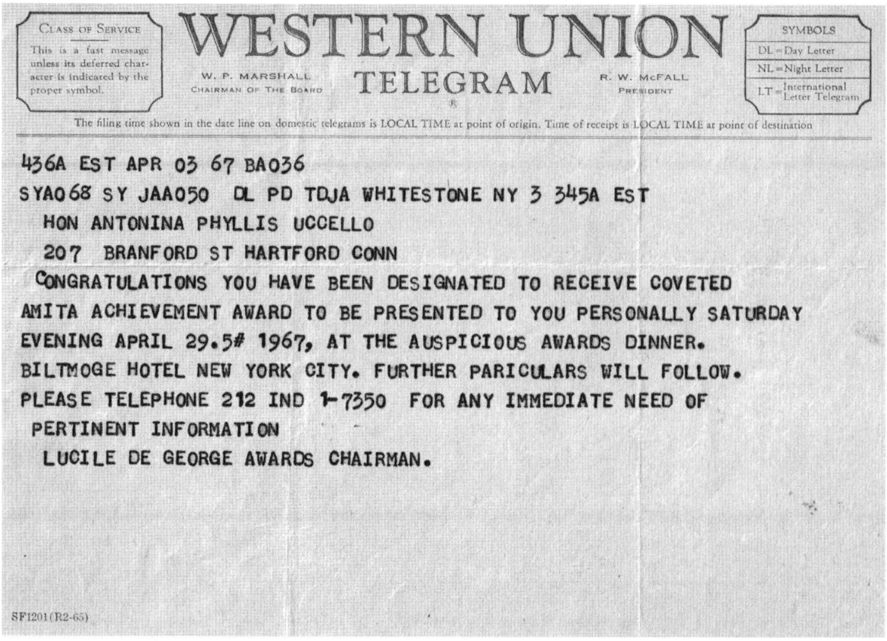

CLASS OF SERVICE
This is a fast message unless its deferred character is indicated by the proper symbol.

WESTERN UNION
TELEGRAM
W. P. MARSHALL, CHAIRMAN OF THE BOARD
R. W. McFALL, PRESIDENT

SYMBOLS
DL=Day Letter
NL=Night Letter
LT=International Letter Telegram

The filing time shown in the date line on domestic telegrams is LOCAL TIME at point of origin. Time of receipt is LOCAL TIME at point of destination

436A EST APR 03 67 BA036
SYA068 SY JAA050 DL PD TDJA WHITESTONE NY 3 345A EST
HON ANTONINA PHYLLIS UCCELLO
207 BRANFORD ST HARTFORD CONN
CONGRATULATIONS YOU HAVE BEEN DESIGNATED TO RECEIVE COVETED AMITA ACHIEVEMENT AWARD TO BE PRESENTED TO YOU PERSONALLY SATURDAY EVENING APRIL 29.5# 1967, AT THE AUSPICIOUS AWARDS DINNER. BILTMOGE HOTEL NEW YORK CITY. FURTHER PARICULARS WILL FOLLOW. PLEASE TELEPHONE 212 IND 1-7350 FOR ANY IMMEDIATE NEED OF PERTINENT INFORMATION
LUCILE DE GEORGE AWARDS CHAIRMAN.

SF1201(R2-65)

The 1967 telegram notifying Ann of her selection for the Amita Award. *Ann Uccello's collection.*

The five sisters at the Amita Award celebration for Ann in 1967. *Ann Uccello's collection.*

city and made it ever more dependent on the state. And now the state is spending (wasting?) billions attempting to lure people back to the central city. It remains to be seen whether these investments will pay off.

In April 1967, Ann was selected to receive the prestigious Amita Award, an annual recognition bestowed on an Italian American woman selected from nominees around the entire country in recognition of her work in government. This was a big deal, as it produced widespread praise and put Ann on the national map. Senator Fauliso introduced a senate resolution praising her. Liutenant Governor Frassinelli sent his personal congratulations, as did Sister Theodore (Saint Joseph College president) and an ailing Mrs. Auerbach.

In July 1967, Hartford was shocked by the riots that took place in the predominantly African American North End, disturbances that resulted in the destruction by fire of a Westland Street supermarket and some other scattered violence. The city council met at length with leaders of the black community, as well as some of the young people who had expressed concern about a number of issues, such as housing, employment and the higher cost of goods in their black neighborhood.

But the issues may not have been so simple or clear cut. The *Courant* report on the incident also highlights the conflict between some of the younger leaders of the black community and some of the older and more established figures. Reverend Battles, for one, expressed his opinion that the problem was not a widespread one; rather, he blamed a dozen people whom he felt should be arrested.

Ann was an active participant in all of the discussions, and the council agreed to one of her ideas: an info-mobile that would be staffed by city staff and employees of the Community Renewal Team. The bus would travel through the North End neighborhood to make people aware of services available at the city level and also to collect complaints about problems and refer them to appropriate city leaders so that corrective action could be taken.

In August 1967, Ann announced plans for a third term. She did so by once again pointing to the need for "leadership that is concerned with the needs of people and not with political power plays."

The talk of the city was the unannounced contest between Kinsella and Ritter, and no one believed that any other candidate had a chance to come in first. In 1965, Kinsella had received over 17,000 votes, with Ritter getting 16,300 and Ann achieving fourth place with some 13,000 votes.

On October 17, 1967, the city of Hartford voters expressed their preferences on the twenty-two candidates seeking office and whittled them down to eighteen. But the real shocker was that Ann finished first, Kinsella

In 1967, the Uccello family listens to radio reports of the Hartford Council primary results in which Ann finished first. *Courtesy of the* Hartford Courant.

second and Ritter a distant third. "If the people of Hartford see fit to elect me Mayor of the city, I won't be afraid of the challenge," stated Ann to Jack Zaiman, *Courant* reporter, who had published an article with the title "Winsome Winner Faces Future."

The November election turned out to be one of the most momentous in the history of the city. For the first time ever, Hartford had elected a woman as

Ann posing in 1967 for one of the many newspapers that came calling to interview the new mayor. *Ann Uccello's collection.*

(HC1) HARTFORD,Conn., Nov.7- LADY MAYOR - Buoyant
with excitement, Ann Uccello accepts congratulations
on her victory as the new mayor of H.rtford. The
Republican candidate had led all opponets in the
October primary. (APWirephoto) pja 32150hwhatz

A happy mayor on the phone in 1967. *AP wire photo.*

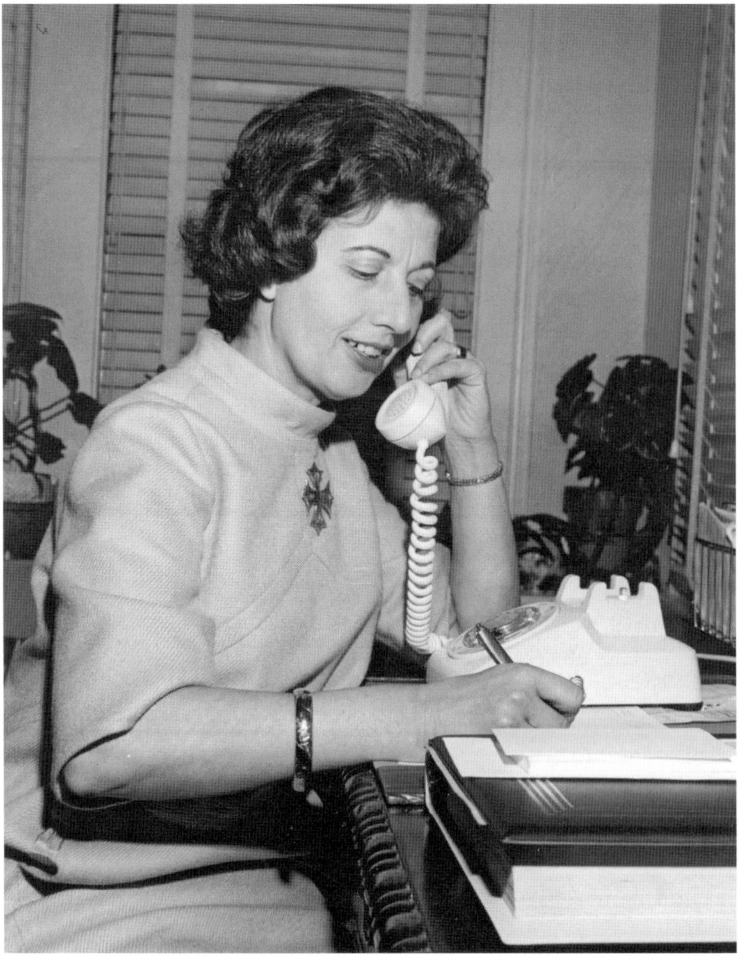

Ann in 1967, answering the many congratulatory calls that inundated the Uccello family following Ann's election to mayor. *An Uccello's collection.*

mayor (first in the state and first in the country insofar as mayor of large cities), and she was a Republican in a city where Democrats outnumbered Republicans by a three-to-one margin. Ann Uccello had surprised even herself—but not Mrs. Auerbach or George Ducharme, both of whom had predicted exactly that outcome years earlier.

Chapter 6

Mayor of Hartford

After the 1967 elections, Ann spent most of the day at home with her family, at least in body if not in spirit; she was on on the phone fielding the many congratulatory calls from friends, relatives, supporters and political leaders. And while many people around her were ecstatic, she was the one to show the least emotion. Her disciplined approach to problem solving and the handling of the duties to be occupied most of her mind.

Twenty-five years after their last mayoral win, Republicans had something to celebrate. The political pundits were stunned that a woman and a Republican in a city dominated by Democrats, the home of John Bailey, had been able to achieve such an objective that not even she believed possible. After such wins, the political speculation begins. "She is a force to be reckoned with statewide," said one analyst, while another predicted she was going to run against Congressman Daddario.

The win was exclusively Ann's win. She had no coattails to ride, and Republicans had actually lost one council member, so Democrats were again six to three in the majority. She won because she was a fresh face who was focused on issues while Democrats continued to fight among themselves. She won with the support of a large Italian American vote, a growing force in local politics.

But winning an election is a lot easier than governing a city where the mayor is only a figurehead and the council is controlled by the opposition party. And it did not take long before the Democrats showed what their strategy would be for the first two years of Ann Uccello's mayoral tenure.

Above: The 1967 swearing-in ceremony as mayor of Hartford. *Ann Uccello's collection.*

Left: Mayor Ann Uccello in 1967. *Ann Uccello's collection.*

Mayor Uccello surrounded by police and fire officials at her 1967 inauguration. *Ann Uccello's collection.*

Ann was sworn in on December 5, 1967. Her inaugural address was one of what we today would call a compassionate conservative. She stated that the city could not wait for federal funds (which were increasingly committed to funding the Vietnam War) to solve the housing crisis in the North End, the site of the riots just a few months back. To do so, she proposed a public-private funding approach that would result in the construction of apartments to then be sold to local residents. She also proposed the building of more

GO-GETTER

PUBLISHED WEEKLY BY AND FOR THE EMPLOYEES OF G. FOX & CO.

Volume XXXIII Number 45 November 10, 1967 HARTFORD, CONNECTICUT

SERVICE... DOING THE RIGHT THING

CONGRATULATIONS ...
ANN UCCELLO

Our Ann Uccello scored two FIRSTS...

FIRST Foxonian to be Mayor-Elect of Hartford!

FIRST woman to be Mayor-Elect of a large Connecticut city!

G. FOX & COMPANY is proud of you!

CHARGE $$$$ $$$$

Assistant Department Manager, Gorton Myers, Collection, left, presents $1.00 bills to Giuseppe Papa, Alterations and Larry Strecker, Purchasing. How many have YOU received. Turn in your applications NOW! Charge (Accounts) can mean cash!

Charge Contest ends tomorrow!
FIRST GRAND PRIZE $300.00
Plus three more grand prizes:

2nd Prize	$200.00
3rd Prize	$150.00
4th Prize	$100.00

JOYCE CICCHETTI, a member of the Junior Executive Training Squad, was a Foxonian for just TWO WEEKS when the letter about her superior customer service arrived. This is what the Plymouth customer had to say..."I recently had the occasion to shop in your store for a dress I needed for a particular social event. I looked in several departments and now wish to call your attention to a particular saleslady in the Miss Sophisticate Shop. The young lady was all one could ask for in good grooming, politeness and in her sincere effort to help me find the right dress. She gave me excellent service. She was not overly aggressive and was honest in her appraisal about how the dresses fitted me and how becoming they were on me. In my opinion, she is a definite asset to your organization and should be commended for her sincere desire to be helpful to your customers."

Peg Servick, Education & Development Director, showed Joyce the letter. Joyce's smile was as wide as our marquee is long. She replied, "I am thrilled and honored to have received such a wonderful letter which proves my classes at Russell Sage and G. FOX were

Please turn to page two.

Peg Servick, E & D Director, extends congratulations to Joyce Cicchetti.

The G. Fox newsletter in 1967 announces a first for the company: one of its employees had been elected mayor. *Ann Uccello's collection.*

training centers within the city to improve the skills of the unemployed. On education, she argued for the speedy consideration and acceptance of long-delayed school construction plans that had been mired in inner council fighting. She argued for a "metropolitan" approach to problem solving but also emphasized that Hartford could not wait on the sidelines until such a system came into place. She believed Hartford civic leaders needed to roll up their sleeves and get to work.

"MISS UCCELLO OFFERS A SOUND PROGRAM" was the headline of the December 7 editorial by the *Courant*, emphasizing the three cornerstones of her plans: training centers, housing built on public-private partnership and the swift construction of new schools. But as the editorial also stated: "She and the Council have their work cut out for them. Hartford will be watching to see what gets accomplished."

It did not take long for the Democrats on the council to show their true colors, and it wasn't pretty.

"ANN'S CONFRERES NOT ALL GENTLEMEN" was the headline of an article dated December 17, 1967, a scant ten days after inauguration. James O'Hara, the *Courant* reporter who authored the piece, said: "Silly pettiness has characterized the behavior of the six-member Democratic majority so far on the newly elected Council." O'Hara described what he defined as "club-car humor" employed by a couple of the council members who made a big show of not knowing how to address the new mayor. One called her "Mrs. Mayor" (and I am sure they all knew she was single), while another called her "Miss Mayor" or "Madame Mayor" in mock confusion. "It was the kind of humor one might find delivered…in the locker room of the Fast Men's Handball Club," according to O'Hara.

Launching the Concentrated Employment Program initiative in 1968. *Ann Uccello's collection.*

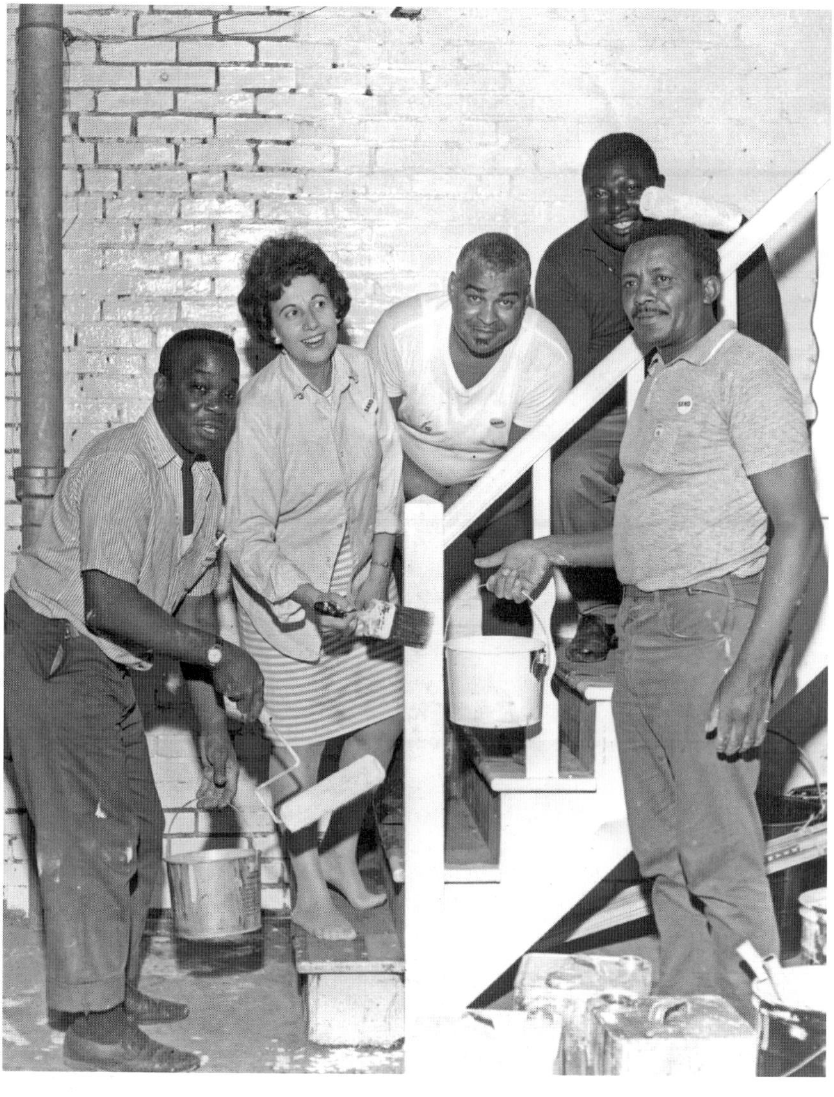

Launching a new housing project at the South Arsenal in 1968—and doing some painting! *Courtesy of the* Hartford Courant.

The Democrats took other actions on more substantive issues that contradicted established policies and even ran contrary to the charter changes approved by the voters but that would not go into effect for another two years. Nope, the Democrats were not going to let a Republican and a woman run their city or even have the appearance of being involved in the process. Their injured pride took precedence over the affairs of the city.

Right: Ann with Engelbert Humperdink in 1969. *Ann Uccello's collection.*

Below: Raising money and visibility for UNICO in 1969. *Ann Uccello's collection.*

The more the Democrats played games, the more voters would trust Ann Uccello as their mayor, and so in this, the Democrats helped create the conditions that led to Ann's success. These tricks certainly failed to faze her. No amount of games or unwarranted criticism would impact Ann's single-minded focus on the business of the people.

When I asked Ann about this name calling and the comments reported in the press, she told me she did not recall any such issues. Yes, she recalls different heated discussions and lots of arguments, especially when Nick Carbone, George Levine and George Athanson were on the council. The one time she did come away personally hurt from a council meeting, an inappropriate and offensive comment was made by a female GOP council member.

The year 1967 drew to a close on a high for the new mayor, the antics of the Democratic Council members not withstanding. "THE YEAR OF THE WOMAN" was the December 31, 1967 headline in the *Hartford Courant*, and Ann Uccello was the leading edge of that movement.

That same Sunday, it had been snowing, and she was returning home from Mass. She received a phone call from a female Hartford resident, and she figured it was someone calling to complain about the snow removal being slow.

The real reason for the call? A picture in the *Hartford Courant*—and the caller wanted to know how could the mayor wear white gloves with the red outfit!

This was still the Christmas season, a special time for Ann and her family, who had been brought up in the customs of Sicily and a strong religious faith, which they practiced for their entire lives. Ann remembers her mother making cookies, *cruspeddi* (light balls of dough deep fried in boiling oil), *torrone* (made of honey, sugar, egg whites and almonds) and *giuggiulena* (sesame seeds and honey). Christmas Eve dinner was the highlight of the entire period, and the Uccello family would be joined by friends and relatives, thus making for quite a crowd.

The clan was having a good time when the doorbell rang, and Ann's mother answered the door. Two boys delivered a Christmas card for the mayor. Ann's mother thanked them and informed them that the mayor was doing the dishes. The card was from John Barber, owner of a bar on Barbour Street and a black community leader.

In January 1968, as Mayor Uccello was riding down Barbour Street with Colin Bennet, a black council member, Ann asked, "Where is John's bar?" They stopped at the bar, and Ann went inside and thanked Mr. Barber for the card, apologizing that she had not written earlier to thank him.

that 1968 is a brilliant year administratively for you and the City of Hartford; one reflecting the love and warmth of the polar star of peace and the Princely Son of Man born under its glow.
John Barber
May it be

The 1967 Christmas card from John Barber to Mayor Ann Uccello. *Ann Uccello's collection.*

Barber and the patrons were "bowled over" by the mayor's visit. This anecdote says so much about Ann and her values—perhaps more effectively than this entire book.

THE JANUARY 1968 TO NOVEMBER 1969 timeframe could have very easily been one of the most productive in the history of Hartford government. It probably was the last real opportunity to make significant changes in policies that could have prevented the long slide into the city's economic downturn.

No, Mayor Uccello was not perfect nor always right, but she was a common sense leader who did her homework and did not like to play political games. Unfortunately, she was confronting a group of council Democrats who would have done anything to stop her from becoming a successful mayor and of winning reelection should she run again. So the issues may have changed, but the story was the same.

The attempt to participate in a new federal program called the Model Cities program was a case in point. In February 1968, the council Democrats elected themselves to the City Demonstration Agency and appointed Deputy Mayor Kinsella as chair while also appointing a former Springfield, Massachusetts administrator to the interim executive director job. This was done without consulting Mayor Uccello, the business community or the neighborhood groups—and most likely in violation of the federal guidelines governing the program.

After many months of debate, the council finally agreed to create a twenty-three-member board made up of civic leaders and neighborhood representatives to be selected by the mayor and the council. In March 1969, the Democratic majority on the council, led by newly appointed council member Nick Carbone, rejected the final four nominees submitted by the mayor because they did not live in Hartford. The Democrats stated that suburban residents had not been involved in the war on poverty and were not qualified to comment on the issue. Mayor Uccello challenged the Democrats to ratify this policy and to pass a resolution stating their claim that you had to be a Hartford resident to be a member of the committee. They had put themselves in a corner.

Nick Carbone and Ann Uccello had only one thing in common: they are both Italian Americans. But their styles could not have been more different, and their politics even more so. Ann was conservative, always behaving in a proper manner, while Nick was liberal and did not mind throwing a political "bomb" to shake up the competition or the issues.

The real reason for the rejection of the four? One nominee, Greater Hartford Chamber past president Bob Mooney, had apparently dared criticize the Democratic council during his retirement speech. It would take another two months before the Democrats finally approved new appointees—including an out-of-towner—so that the commission could start working. Their deadline was October 1969, and at risk was some $200 million.

In a June 25, 1969 editorial, the *Courant* stated, "After a two-month-long demonstration of partisan spite, the Democratic majority of the Hartford

Common Council has permitted the approval of the last nominations to the twenty-three-member City Demonstration Agency."

While this was going on, the mayor was also fighting charges of being against helping drug users by opposing a drug rehab center proposed by Councilmen Athanson and Carbone. The proposal called for granting $20,000 to Alpis Corporation. Mayor Uccello pointed out that this proposal had several problems, starting with not knowing about the Alpis Corporation's mission, its directors were not identified and the city manager and corporation counsel had no information about Alpis.

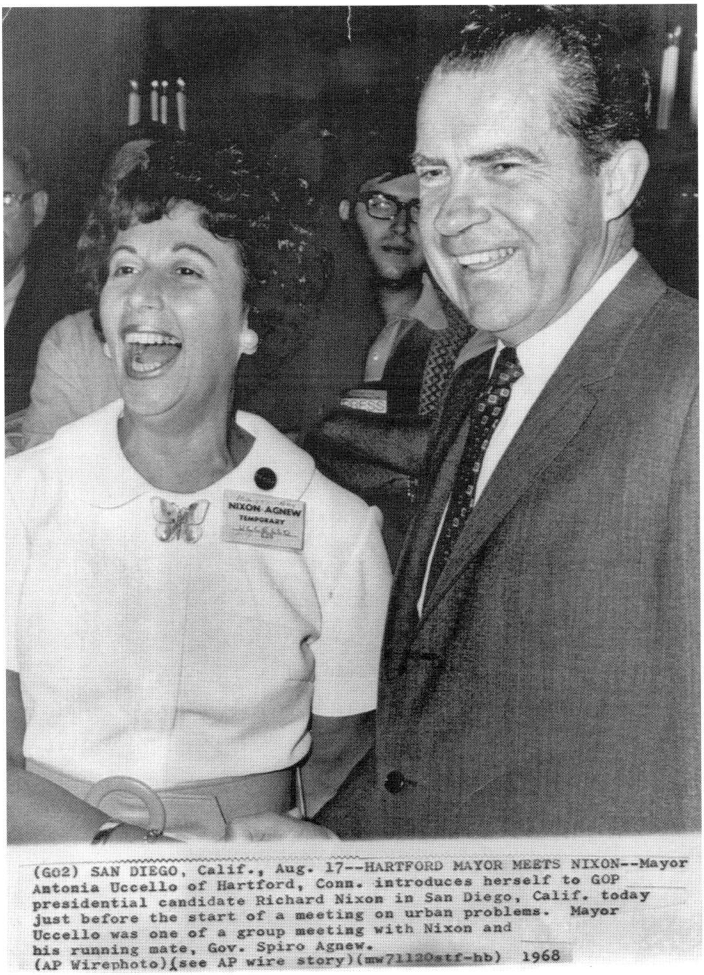

NIXON AGNEW
TEMPORARY
(G02) SAN DIEGO, Calif., Aug. 17--HARTFORD MAYOR MEETS NIXON--Mayor
Antonia Uccello of Hartford, Conn. introduces herself to GOP
presidential candidate Richard Nixon in San Diego, Calif. today
just before the start of a meeting on urban problems. Mayor
Uccello was one of a group meeting with Nixon and
his running mate, Gov. Spiro Agnew.
(AP Wirephoto)(see AP wire story)(mw71120stf-hb) 1968

Ann in 1968 with candidate Richard Nixon in San Diego for a conference on housing. *Ann Uccello's collection.*

She decried what she called the "irresponsible and highly questionable" conduct of Councilman Athanson. Was she opposed to drug rehab, as then charged by the Democrats? Of course not—but she was appalled that money was being spent without all the issues being studied and outlined or the appropriate legal steps taken to form the legal infrastructure of this new entity.

Mayor Uccello was not shy about criticizing Republicans with equal candor. In 1968, GOP presidential nominee Richard Nixon invited her to San Diego for a parley on urban problems. Upon her return, she declared the meeting "disappointing"—the promised discussion with Nixon had never taken place, and the whole thing had turned out to be nothing more than a photo opportunity organized by the Nixon campaign.

In 1970, President Nixon organized a similar event in Indianapolis. Mayor Uccello was invited again and told the caller that, yes, she would participate but that she expected to speak and was not interested in another San Diego–type appearance. President Nixon opened the meeting with some brief remarks and a pointed comment: "Mayor Uccello did not have time to speak last year in San Diego, and so the floor is hers." Ann was both stunned and ready—stunned to be called to the "carpet" but ready with material on hand to discuss the many substantive issues facing cities like Hartford.

Ann in 1970 in Indianapolis with President Nixon for another conference on housing. *Ann Uccello's collection.*

In 1968, Mayor Uccello was burning the candle at both ends, and it eventually would catch up to her. In November of that year, she was admitted to Saint Francis Hospital complaining of pains in the abdomen area. Nothing was found, and no recurrence ever took place, but there is no doubt that the stress of the job was at the very least a contributing factor.

The games being played by the Democrats were taking their toll, but real life events were challenging Mayor Uccello in ways that few people could have ever predicted.

The assassination of civil rights leader Martin Luther King in April 1968 unleashed riots in the black communities across the country, and Hartford was not spared. Mayor Uccello won enormous praise from all, friends and opponents, for the courageous and direct way she handled the situation. She spent countless hours at city hall coordinating the various responses, but even more importantly, she went to the neighborhoods affected by the riots and talked to the local community.

She had no hesitation in doing so, and years of being visible, engaged and in contact with the black community gave her credibility. She knew many of the black leaders from earlier years, and people respected her call to address the housing problems and other issues identified by the 1967 riots. Just two months earlier, she had initiated a tour of the living conditions in the North End and had called for forceful and coordinated actions from agencies, churches, volunteers and welfare workers, as well tenants and landlords, to correct the brutal living conditions of the poor minorities.

Still, walking out of a police cruiser at 4:00 a.m., a petite woman in the midst of destruction holding the hard hat police had instructed her to wear, took lots of courage. She approached groups of people hanging around, and she would ask questions and answer in a low but firm voice. At one point in time, as described by Barbara Carlson in an April 6 article in the *Courant*, she was surrounded by one hundred people. Some jeered while others invited the crowd to "cool it." One man greeted her, saying, "You are the mayor? I expected someone a lot bigger."

When a young man told her she had nerve to come to their streets, a white bystander said, "It's her city." Ann corrected him, saying, "It's *our* city."

One of the most iconic pictures of those days would be taken just a few hours later on the steps of city hall. It shows a diminutive Mayor Uccello answering questions and surrounded by black youth. Several hundred students from Hartford Public High had marched to Saint Joseph Cathedral and then to city hall, where, after a few minutes, they were met by Mayor Uccello. They carried on a civil discussion in which the students outlined their grievances, and the mayor answered and promised to help.

In 1968, Mayor Uccello speaks to a group of black students protesting the assassination of Martin Luther King. *Ann Uccello's collection.*

Later that year, she would be asked about those violent days and whether she was afraid. Of course she was afraid, but once again, she had her secret weapon with her: her rosary beads.

Two other important events were also going on in '68: the Vietnam War and related protests, coupled with the election for U.S. president. In October of that year, Hartford received a visit from Spiro Agnew, and a reception was held at the Statler Hilton overlooking Bushnell Park. Mayor Uccello was introducing Mr. Agnew when she looked out the window and saw Vietnam War protesters milling around at the park. Pointing to the protesters, she called them "the Benedict Arnolds of our generation," a remark met by thundering applause.

The year 1968 also produced some lighter moments. In February, Mayor Uccello began to receive fan mail; her picture had been reproduced in newspapers around the country, and some people were contacting her. Harry from Pennsylvania wrote of how attractive he found the new mayor. A man from Louisiana wrote that he could not understand how someone as good-looking and intelligent as she had remained unmarried and suggested that it must be the fault of the local gentlemen. An inmate at a state jail sent her a song he had written.

In June of that same year, Mayor Uccello led a small delegation to the U.S. Conference of Mayors being held in Chicago. John Lindsay, the then legendary mayor of New York City, was chairing the event, and he grew so incensed at the solutions to city problems being outlined by Mayor Uccello that he relinquished the gavel and took the floor to forcefully rebut her.

The Chicago trip also included a foray into social life—unusual for the mayor. She went out with a few colleagues for dinner and then went to the nightclub district of Chicago, where they had a good time. At about 4:00 a.m., they left the club and took a walk to Lake Michigan, and taking off their shoes, they dipped their toes in the lake. The confrontation with Lindsay had taken place on three or four hours of sleep.

A reporter was also a member of the Uccello party that evening, but nothing was ever written or said about the night out. The press mostly loved Ann, and especially so the *Hartford Courant*, which had endorsed her for mayor.

The year 1969 was no less stressful, and it also was a municipal election year. This time, the new mayor would carry enhanced powers brought about by charter changes approved in 1967, thus ensuring that the Democrats would do all in their power to make sure Ann Uccello would not be mayor.

In addition to the ongoing battles with Athanson, Carbone and Ritter (the model cities commission, the rehab center, how to best deal with lead paint, etc.), Ann had to once again deal with large riots that brought the city to its knees and forced city administrators to impose a 7:00 p.m. curfew.

In June 1969, the city experienced two days of rioting, but it was the September riots that shook the city to its core and taxed Ann's capabilities to the limit.

Mayor Uccello was in Maine for the Labor Day weekend. The trouble started the evening of Labor Day when a large group of Puerto Ricans gathered at the firehouse at the corner of Belden and Main Streets to protest an article in the *Hartford Times* in which a fireman was quoted as calling Puerto Ricans "pigs." Over the next five days, more than five hundred people would be arrested, mostly for looting or breaking the curfew imposed by the city on Tuesday morning. In just two days, firemen answered 179 fire calls. More than seventy businesses, most of them in the North End of the city, were burned or looted. Many innocent North End residents were driven out of their homes by the fumes of tear gas used by police to disperse the crowds.

Ann in 1968 with Councilman Nicholas Carbone, discussing the response to the riots that followed the assassination of Martin Luther King. *Ann Uccello's collection.*

Mayor Uccello, who had returned to the city as soon as possible and witnessed the riots firsthand, declared the state of emergency over on Monday, September 8, while the curfew had been lifted the prior Saturday. Ann's reaction to the riots was forceful:

> *The violence, looting and burning that enveloped our City last week must not be repeated. This was the second such outbreak in three months, and my fellow citizens, I tell you quite frankly, the City cannot stand another. The criminal activity we witnessed this past week has brought hardship to thousands of people throughout Hartford. Not only did innocent people suffer from the forceful action that was taken to stop the disorders, but these same people can no longer avail themselves of the necessary services that were supplied by the drugstores and other retail establishments that were destroyed last week. Those militants*

> *who choose violence to gain their objectives hurt no one but the very people, they profess to help.*

She argued that their actions had damaged the very people the protesters were trying to support, as grocery stores and drugstores in the North End were now having problems getting deliveries of food and medicine.

> *Many reasons have been advanced as the cause of these riots, but there is absolutely no justification for this type of activity. Poor housing conditions or uncomplimentary newspaper articles are no excuse for criminal action, and those who say they are do a disservice to the total community and to the people whose conditions they wish to improve. I can sympathize with the frustration that results from living in slum conditions and from being subjected to prejudice, but it does not justify looting and burning. If everyone were allowed to take out his frustrations in this manner, the result would be anarchy. Our whole society would be torn apart in bloodshed and chaos.*
>
> *Let's face it. The major part of the criminal activity that was perpetrated upon our community last week was not done by people protesting poor social conditions. An excellent library catering to the needs of minority youngsters would not have been burned down if this were so. No, this activity was instigated by agitators and carried out by hoodlums looking for an opportunity to loot and burn, who would steal no matter what the social conditions.*

Ann went on to argue for a forceful legal response to the actions of the looters.

> *A slap on the wrist is not the way to say "Don't do it again." The punishment must fit the crime, and a small fine or suspended sentence is not the way to stop those who would loot and burn or exploit the poor, or defy authority.*
>
> *The Courts must do their part in protecting the community. The right of peace-loving people in our City to protection of their lives and property is just as important as the rights of those who commit these crimes against the community.*

Her speech also recognized some of the long-term social trends then developing, such as the move to the suburbs, and raised issues that are timely today:

> *Unless peace and tranquility are permanently restored to our City, there will be a mass exodus of middle-income people so that the core city will then become the exclusive home of the poor and the underprivileged and no one will be left to help. This fact should be recognized by the suburbs as well as the city, because the suburbs, economically and culturally, revolve around and depend upon the core city. If the city does not survive, neither will the suburbs.*
>
> *With the wealthy moving to the suburbs the city can no longer solve its problems alone. We must have help from the very people who depend upon our survival. Artificial and geographic barriers must be broken down, and surrounding towns must absorb some of the population of the inner city. If necessary, the State must step in to help in the elimination of obstacles that may arise. This, of course, must be accompanied by improvement and expansion of mass transportation facilities to enable the poor who move to the suburbs to be sufficiently mobile to be able to travel to and from their jobs.*

Ann concluded her speech as follows:

> *And so my fellow citizens, in the aftermath of the tragedy that struck Hartford last week, I ask that all of us reflect. Those who live beyond our city limits, who could open their minds and their hearts, those officials, businessmen and citizens who have too often substituted words and platitudes for performance, those who are charged with dispensing justice for the community as well as the individual, those who seek political power at the expense of their own people, those who choose to obtain their goals through militant action, those who permit their children to join in the violence and destruction…reflect, and then walk or drive slowly through the gutted, ravaged streets of Hartford…and as the tragic scene unfolds, let us reflect not on what has been done, but on what we can do, what we must do to see that it never happens again. In the measure of our respect for the rights of others, sense of justice, personal responsibility and sincerity of our belief in the brotherhood of man, we will find the answers.*

Ann's hard work as the mayor had not gone unnoticed to the editorial board of the *Courant*, which on October 26, 1969, endorsed her candidacy to a second term as mayor. In endorsing her candidacy for mayor, the *Hartford Courant* stated, "Perhaps most important of all, it seems to us, is the streak of common sense that shows through her action and words…She calls for a fair shake for all citizens: she does not jump up and down and scream 'law and order.'"

The editorial concluded, "Hartford needs leadership, the type personified by the mayor who goes out at night to the scene of disorders on the streets and who will talk quietly with the disaffected. Hartford also needs intelligence and honesty, and common sense, in its City Hall. All of these qualities we believe Ann Uccello has demonstrated."

Ann's father died on October 3, 1969. He had been in ill health for years and had not participated in nor was perhaps fully aware of all that his daughter was facing and accomplishing. Ann had spent countless hours in his Albany Avenue shoemaker shop, making deliveries to customers, bringing her father lunch and walking home together, like the time when

To Ann Uccello
With best wishes,
Ronald Reagan

Ann in 1967 with Governor Ronald Reagan of California in Hartford for a fundraiser. *Ann Uccello's collection.*

In 1968, Governor Nelson Rockfeller of New York was in Hartford for a fundraiser. *Ann Uccello's collection.*

she consoled him about the teasing he was getting from a "friend" about not having any sons.

The riots and the death of her father would have been more than most people could handle. But Mayor Uccello was also in a fight for reelection.

The year 1969 was going to represent a turning point in the city electoral system: for the first time since 1945, the political parties would be forced to select a candidate for mayor, and the job had the benefit of expanded powers. Democrats were out to avenge their 1967 defeat and stop the Uccello bandwagon.

Ann surprised no one when, in July 1969, she declared her candidacy to be the mayor and run for reelection. She had a small but unified GOP backing her.

Could she win again? Jack Zaiman, the famed political *Courant* writer, concluded that yes, she could win again because she had caught on with voters, but the three-to-one voter registration deficit would not be easily overcome.

Democrats, as usual, did not coalesce around a single candidate. State senator Joseph Fauliso had become the apparent choice to unify the Democrats and to sap the Uccello strength in the Italian American vote. According to Ann, Fauliso declined, saying that he would never do that to Ann's parents, of whom he was a close friend and whom he admired.

Joseph Fauliso, state senate president, was the first one to introduce resolutions in the state senate in praise of Ann's accomplishments. He was a friend of the family and a gentleman.

In August, the Hartford Democrats endorsed Joseph Adinolfi for mayor. However, Deputy Mayor George B. Kinsella, also a Democrat, indicated that he would run as an independent. Wilbur Smith, a leader of the black

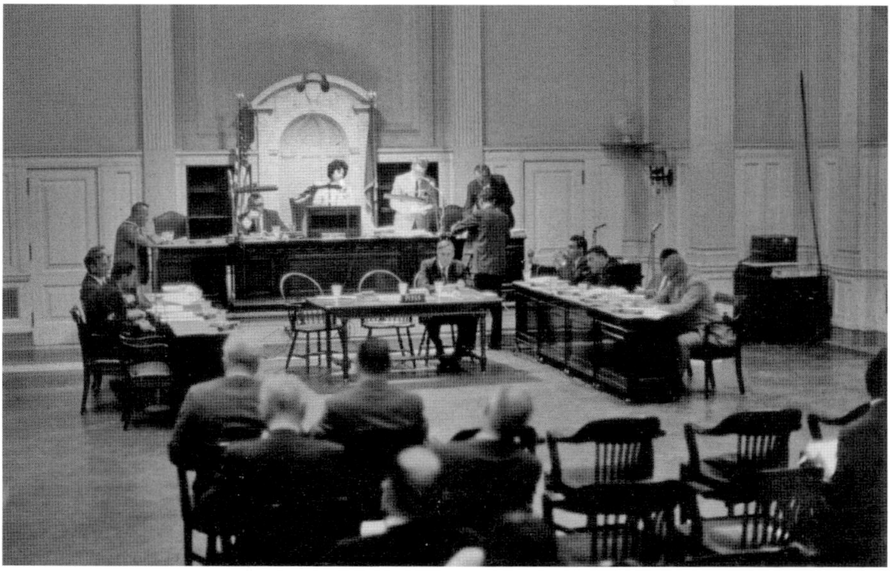

Mayor Uccello presiding over a town council meeting in 1969. *Ann Uccello's collection.*

community, would join the competition, representing the Liberal Party and thus setting up a four-way contest.

From a political strategy standpoint, the election of '69 posed new challenges for the campaign. The GOP had decided that all candidates would get the same amount of money and the same size poster. So George Ducharme had another great idea, again while at church: Ann was going to go door-to-door to as many as possible of the small businesses in the city, introducing herself and asking the owners to place the poster in a visible place. This step helped Ann in two ways: she met one-on-one many of the city's small business owners, and a lot of them did put the poster up in their stores—not necessarily because they agreed with the mayor on every position but because they respected her hard work, honesty and sincerity.

The riots in September 1969 would dominate the election issues, while the death of the mayor's father in October brought about a short "ceasefire" in the daily give and take. Ann shared with me that some members of the family—though neither her sisters nor mother—felt she should have quit the race. To her, that was unthinkable. Her commitment to the city, to the issues she had worked so long and hard for, to her values of work and faith—no, those values demanded that she stay and fight.

The election count was indeed as close as predicted, but Mayor Uccello beat Democratic mayoral candidate Adinolfi by just over five hundred votes and was thus reelected mayor. The house on Branford Street where she lived with her mother and older sister was the site of their happy but subdued victory party—after all, her father had passed away a short month earlier.

"Will Ann Uccello Be Able to Deal with Democrats?" was the lead editorial on November 9 in the *Courant*. The editorial concluded that since she had considerable political skills, the next few months would prove most interesting.

Mayor Uccello had scored another impressive personal win, and speculation about her political future (at her victory speech she was welcomed by shouts of "Ann for governor!") would begin at once. But the balance of power in Hartford had not changed. The Democrats retained their six-to-three advantage over the GOP, and more battles appeared to lie ahead.

How did Ann pull off this miracle? The analysis of *Courant* reporter James O'Hara is spot on: "For one thing she has created an image of integrity and hard work in her two terms on the Council…Ms. Uccello also had a good organization behind her." "It looked like there was one of Ann Uccello's sisters at every polling station in the city," complained a Democrat organizer.

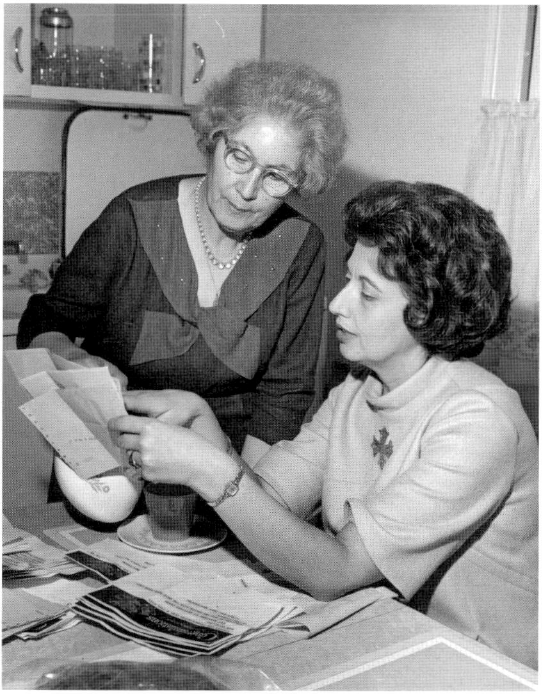

Right: Mayor elect Ann Uccello reviews congratulatory telegrams with her mother in 1969. *Ann Uccello's collection.*

Below: The entire Uccello family in a subdued celebration of the 1969 win. Ann's father had died one month earlier. *Ann Uccello's collection.*

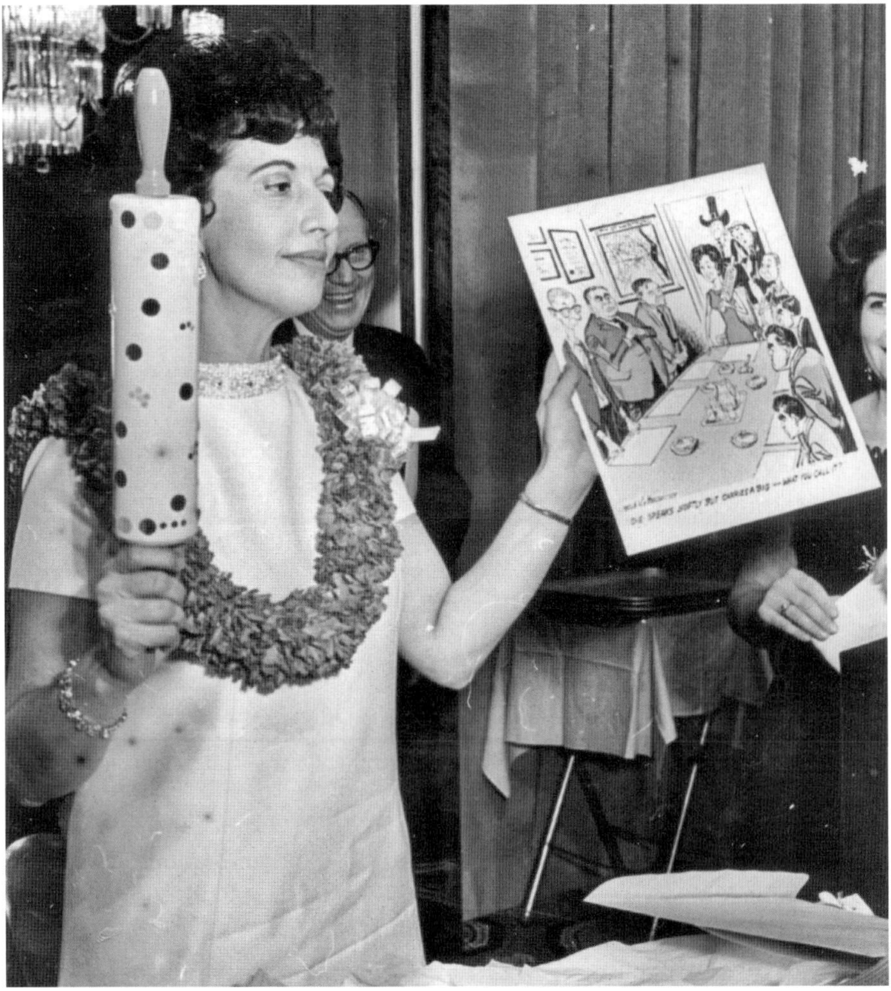

A 1967 *Hartford Times* cartoon captures the new order at the Hartford City Council. *Ann Uccello's collection.*

The year 1969 was a momentous one in the history of Hartford and indeed the entire country. The Vietnam War had split the country as never before or since. The assassinations of Martin Luther King and Robert Kennedy in 1968 had unleashed a wave of protests, riots and violence that was still reverberating in 1969. An era of permissiveness, best represented by the San Francisco hippies and drug users, was slowly coming to an end.

Two days of riots in June 1969 were met by swift declaration of emergency and a curfew. For the city of Hartford, 1969 may have represented the

A 1969 *Hartford Times* cartoon shows who was still on top in Hartford. *Ann Uccello's collection.*

beginning of an irreversible exodus on the part of middle-income families toward the suburbs, changing the character of the city.

A *Courant* article published on June 16 captures the moment best. It is the story of Eugene Interlandi, a cobbler who had operated a shoe repair store in the Albany Avenue area for almost forty years.

In the 1930s, Albany Avenue was a mix of Italians, Jews and blacks living together. Mayor Uccello's own father had a similar shop also on Albany

Life at city hall in 1967 for the incoming mayor, as seen by the same cartoonist for the *Hartford Times. Ann Uccello's collection.*

Avenue, and Ann would make deliveries to clients' homes until late at night without fear for her personal safety.

By 1969, Mr. Interlandi was but one of a handful of non-black shop owners left in the area, and now he was fearful, according to the article. His glass storefront window had been smashed and his store looted. His local friends called him to tell him of the damage, and he went to Capen Street to find indescribable destruction. For a while, the presence of police cars outside his store gave him a sense of protection, but soon those cars were off to the next scene of violence, and Mr. Interlandi was left alone.

In the last few years, Mr. Interlandi had grown fearful of the teenagers who walked the streets of the neighborhood: they would harass him, they would shoplift and they would throw insults at him and his wife. And now

Reelection campaign literature for Mayor Uccello in 1969. *Ann Uccello's collection.*

here he was alone with dozens of young marauders filing in his store and looting all they could find, his pleas to stop met only by taunts and threats.

A few days after the event, he met Mayor Uccello at her office and recounted the story. He had had enough and would not go back to the North End again. One can only imagine what Mayor Uccello, whose father was a shoemaker for over thirty years on Albany Avenue, must have felt.

Chapter 7

A Second Term and a Run for Congress

Ann Uccello's reelection to mayor was big news, but it would soon be replaced on the pages of the local papers by the upcoming 1970 state elections for governor, senator and, of course, the congressional seats. Ann's victory in the Democrat-controlled city of Hartford—although not as large as had been expected—coupled with a state poll showing her as one of the most favored politicians with statewide appeal, made sure her name was being mentioned almost daily next to one of those positions. Would she run for governor? Would she run for senator? Would she run for the congressional seat in the First District?

Mayor Uccello went about her business of mayor with new enhanced powers (she could veto council resolutions, and she had much more say on the budget). Her second inaugural address did not produce grandiose new initiatives but was more a restatement of the 1967 priorities: housing for the North End, a larger police force and a prudent budget.

The "loyal" opposition also had not changed, and at the last council meeting of the 1967 term, the Democrats passed a resolution creating a department of insurance over the objection of Mayor Uccello and city manager Eli Freedman. They could not risk waiting until the new session had begun and give the mayor the opportunity to veto the resolution, a veto that they most likely could not override.

The tone had been set and would not change for the 1970 term. Democrats refused to approve the mayor's recommendation to increase the police force from 434 to 500—at least not when she proposed it in

In 1968, a confident Mayor Uccello looks out over the Hartford skyline from the incomplete top floor of the Bushnell Towers. *Ann Uccello's collection.*

This 1969 photograph at Bradley Airport depicts the "christening" of an American Airline baby jet named Hartford. *Ann Uccello's collection.*

Mayor Uccello attending an ice cream party at a children's camp in 1970. *Courtesy of the* Hartford Courant.

The 1970 Conference of Mayors in Washington, D.C. Ann is pictured with Representative Bob Giaimo to her left and San Francisco mayor Joseph Alioto at far right. *Ann Uccello's collection.*

December 1969 and again in early 1970. The Democratic council eventually would vote to increase the police force to 505, 5 more than requested by Mayor Uccello.

City manager Eli Freedman proposed a 1970 budget of $89 million, some 20 percent higher than the year before and requiring an increase in the mill rate from 64.9 to 77.7. It represented the third year running that the city was proposing a budget reflecting a 15 percent increase in taxes each year—not exactly the recipe needed to retain and expand the economic base, not to mention the impact on the middle-income families who saw their tax bills soar.

There would be the ongoing battles over nominations to commissions. One took center stage in 1970. Mayor Uccello nominated Sister Theodore, retired president of Saint Joseph College, to replace Noel Tomas on the Commission on Aging. Democrats, led by Athanson and Carbone, were incensed over the appointment and did all they could to defeat it.

It took over a month, but the appointment was finally approved by a vote of five to four, with Democrats DeLucco and Heslin joining the Republicans

Mayor Uccello received the prestigious Paca Award for outstanding service in government in 1969. *Ann Uccello's collection.*

Right: The 1969 retirement party for Art McGinley, legendary *Hartford Times* sports reporter. *Ann Uccello's collection.*

Below: In 1969, *Hartford Times* staff surprised the mayor with a birthday cake, but the little boy enjoyed it more than anyone from the look on his face. *Ann Uccello's collection.*

Celebrating the fiftieth anniversary of the founding of Connecticut Natural Gas Company in 1970. *Ann Uccello's collection.*

to make the approval possible. Of course, the process had taken a month, more "blood" had been spilled and more battles fought. Any chance of working together for the common good of the city appeared distant at best.

Speaking at a meeting organized by the Greater Hartford Chamber of Commerce in February 1970, Mayor Uccello was prophetic in her remarks: the middle class was leaving the city, the newcomers were low-income families requiring more support from the city and the process was accelerating so rapidly that she felt the "city could not cope with it."

In June 1970, Mayor Uccello was in Denver participating in the annual U.S. Conference of Mayors when she was invited to be a guest on *Meet the Press* by legendary host Lawrence Spivak. She would be one of six mayors (and the only female mayor) from around the country discussing, in a nonpolitical way, issues facing the cities.

It's not clear who on the panel fired the first political shot, but when Nixon's policies and his spending money on the Vietnam War were discussed, Ann was firm in the defense of Nixon. The president had inherited the war

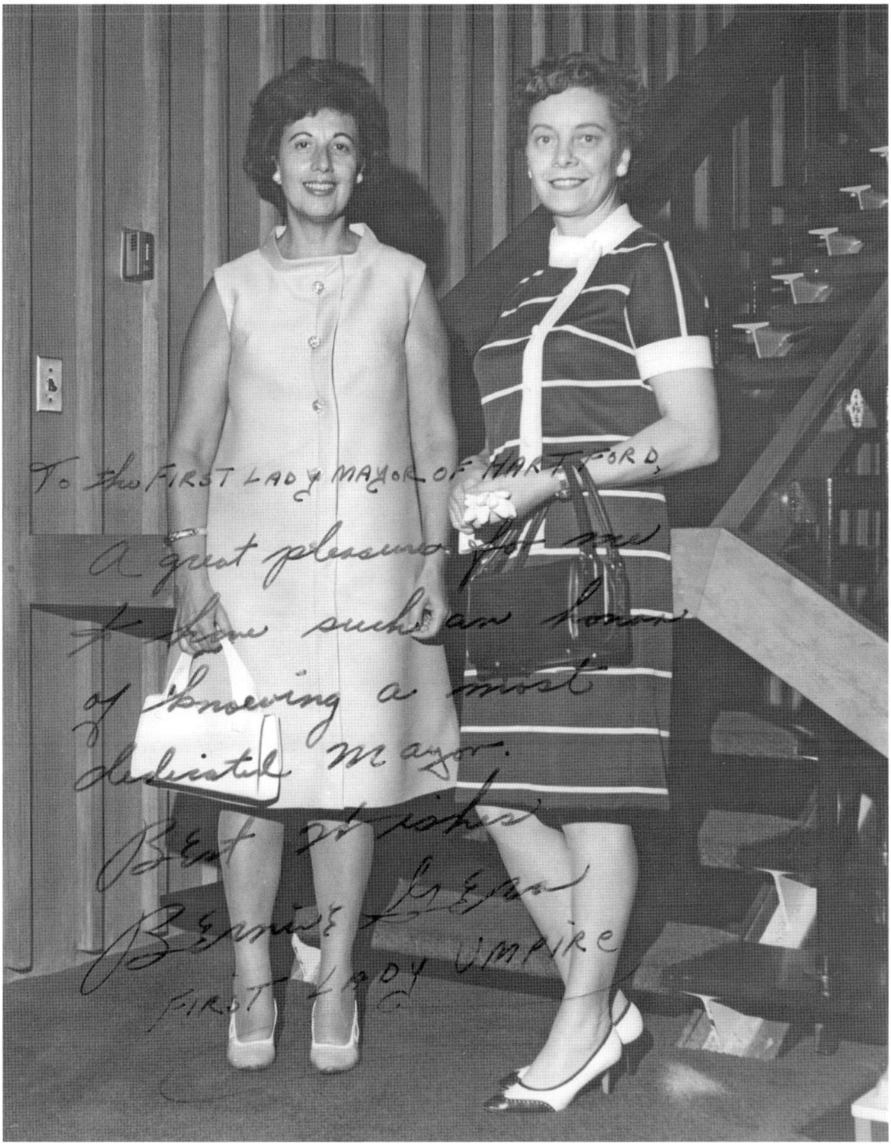

In 1969, the first female mayor met the first female umpire. *Ann Uccello's collection.*

from a Democratic administration and was trying his best to wind it down while allocating more money to the cities. Mayor Lugar of Indianapolis, the only other Republican mayor on the panel, pointed out that the federal government was spending more money than ever on city needs.

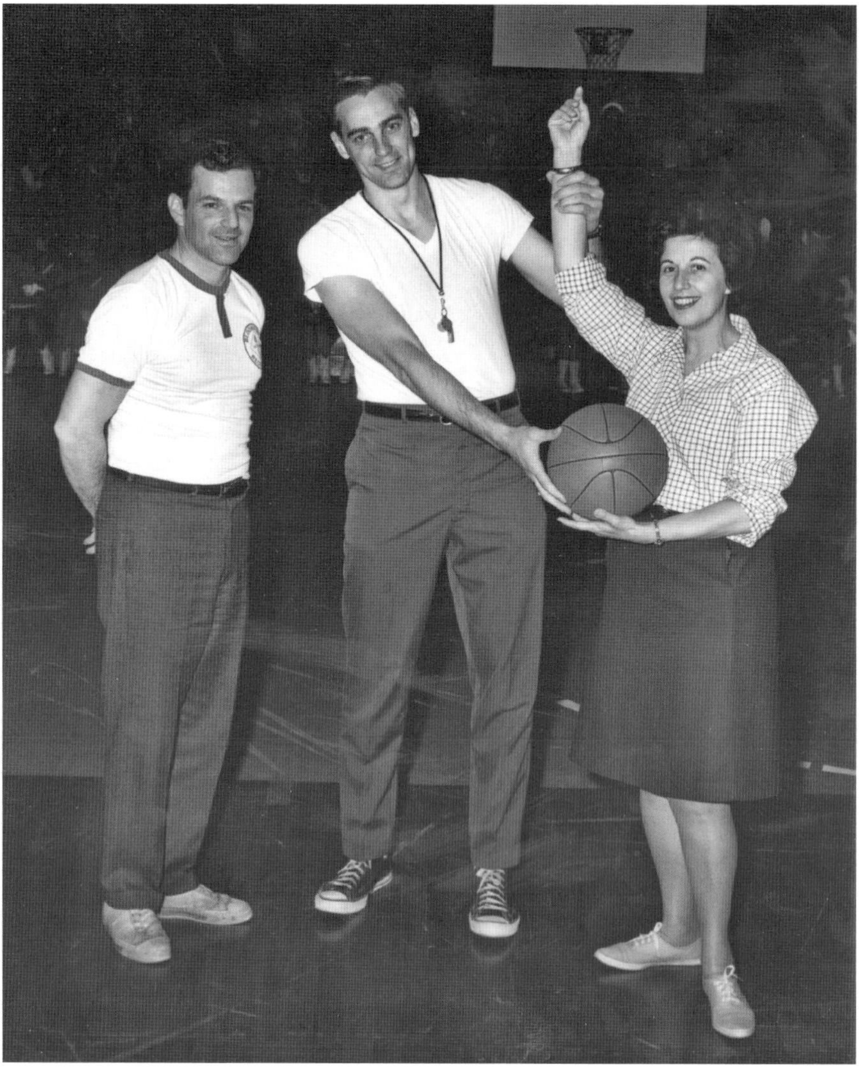

Mayor Uccello defeats Mayor Lewis Rome of Bloomfield in a basketball shootout in 1969. *Ann Uccello's collection.*

Her TV appearance received glowing comments from people around the country who would write the mayor letters of praise in the days following. Most of those letters praised her intellect, ability to articulate the issues and her defense of President Nixon.

Some were not as kind. One lady told her that while at first she was glad to see a woman with both looks and brains, she grew disappointed at

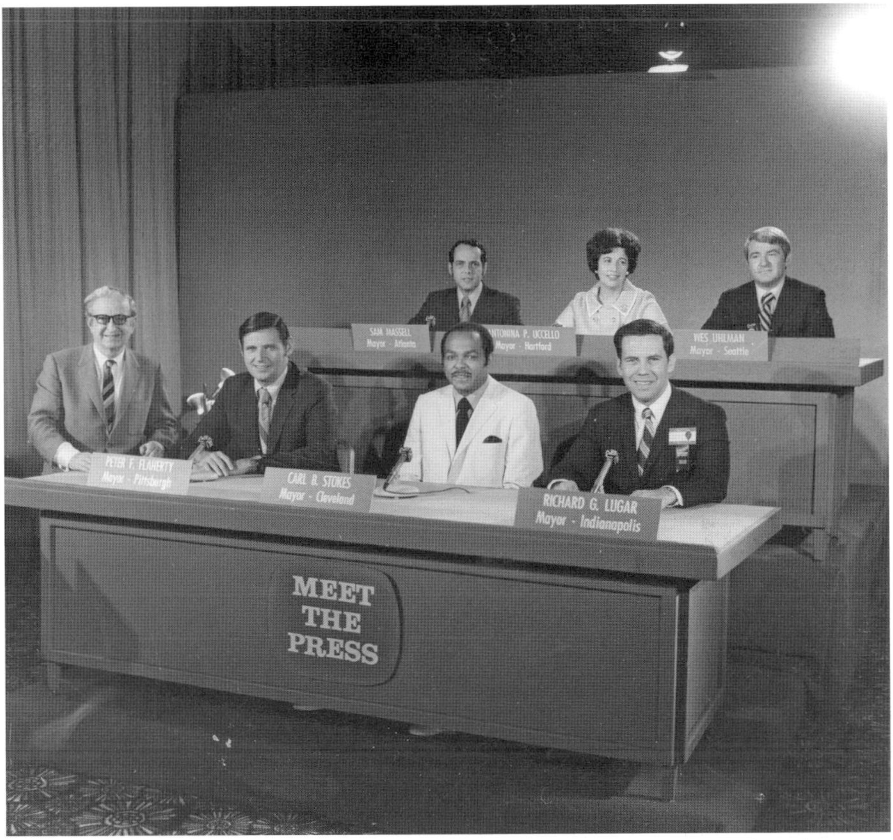

Ann presented a strong defense of President Nixon on *Meet the Press* in 1970. *Ann Uccello's collection.*

Ann's mannerisms "in throwing your head around…to say nothing of your affected head pose in the group picture." She advised Ann to "drop that childish coyness."

One anonymous "admirer" wrote that she was "a stinking dagos" and compared her to New Jersey mayor Addonzio, who was convicted of taking bribes. He went on to say that Ann was probably a mafiosa, and so were her parents, signed "Disgusted Citizen." Ouch.

Upon her return to Hartford, Ann's attention was once again focused on the political choice that would decide her future. She had come to conclude that she would like to run for governor, senator being a second choice and representative of the First Congressional District a distant third. The problem is that she was being outmaneuvered at every corner by male politicians who had no interest in naming a woman to the top of a statewide ticket.

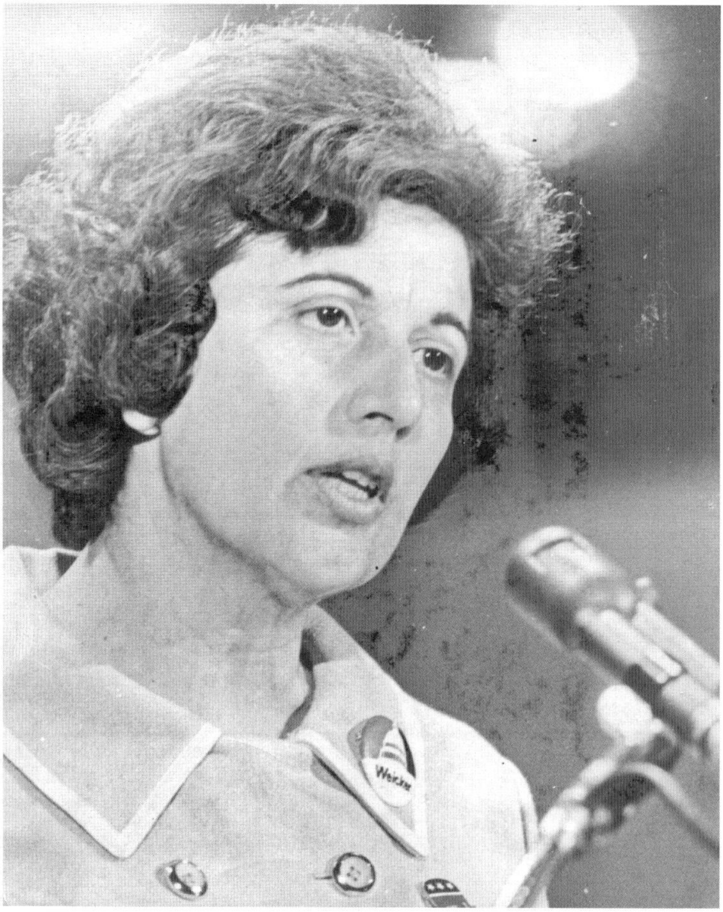

Delivering a convention speech in 1970 endorsing Lowell Weicker for Senate. *Ann Uccello's collection.*

The process started with a call from Howard Hausman, state GOP chair, inviting Ann to lunch to discuss the situation. After a few brief niceties, Mr. Hausman came to the point of the lunch: would Ann be interested in a commissioner position in a Meskill administration? Ann was furious. "Howard," she said to him, "this is an insult. If I had been the male mayor of Hartford, we would not be here to talk about a commissioner's job."

Ann also recalls meetings with Weicker and Thomas Meskill. Weicker informed Ann that he was running for the senate and that he would primary if he did not get the nomination. But he did say that he would not primary if Ann were the nominee. He asked for her support and also asked that she place his name in nomination at the state convention. She did and sent a letter to Weicker and all convention delegates with a warm endorsement.

On another occasion, Mayor Uccello was having lunch with Meskill, who was asking for her endorsement of his gubernatorial candidacy. A startled waitress came to the table to inform the mayor that she had a call from the White House. Ann answered the call and was told that President Nixon would like to speak to her and when would she be back at her office. In half an hour was the reply.

Thirty minutes later, the phone rang, and it was indeed President Nixon, who, after some niceties, asked Mayor Uccello to run for the First District Congressional seat. Mayor Uccello was flattered but said she wanted to think about and would get back to the president the next day.

She did, and she accepted the challenge. "I run to win," she informed the president, who pledged unlimited support in her campaign.

Ann recounted these facts to me in 2014. I pointed out to her that she appeared to have been outflanked by her opponents and by their proactive, aggressive moves for the position. Of course, she did have a city to run, but Ann also lacked the contacts at the State GOP Committee that could have been leveraged to allow her to claim the gubernatorial or senatorial nomination. She did not have a Brian Gaffney, the GOP operative who spearheaded the Meskill drive to the gubernatorial nomination and election victory. She was a woman in a man's world.

The GOP lost a chance to nominate an Italian American woman for governor, a feat that a short four years later the Democrats would accomplish by nominating Ella Grasso, the first female governor in Connecticut and the first female governor in the country to be elected on her own merits.

Her family was perhaps also one of the factors that may have held Ann back. George Ducharme recalled a meeting at the Uccellos' residence when the issue was being discussed, and while he was in favor of a run for the Senate, Ann's mother and sisters expressed doubts about the ability to raise enough money and to be able to come up with the statewide organization to win. The family prevailed, and Ann would run for Congress.

In June 1970, Ann declared her candidacy for the First District. Another GOP candidate for the position withdrew, and Ann was in. However, city business would require her full attention.

If elected, she pledged to work to obtain more money for urban mass transit; she declared that the economic development of downtown Hartford and the success of the Civic Center demanded new approaches to mass transit and less reliance on automobiles. She attacked the state Democrats

Above: The 1970 announcement of her candidacy to the First Congressional District. *Ann Uccello's collection.*

Left: Ann's campaign staff for the 1970 congressional race. *Ann Uccello's collection.*

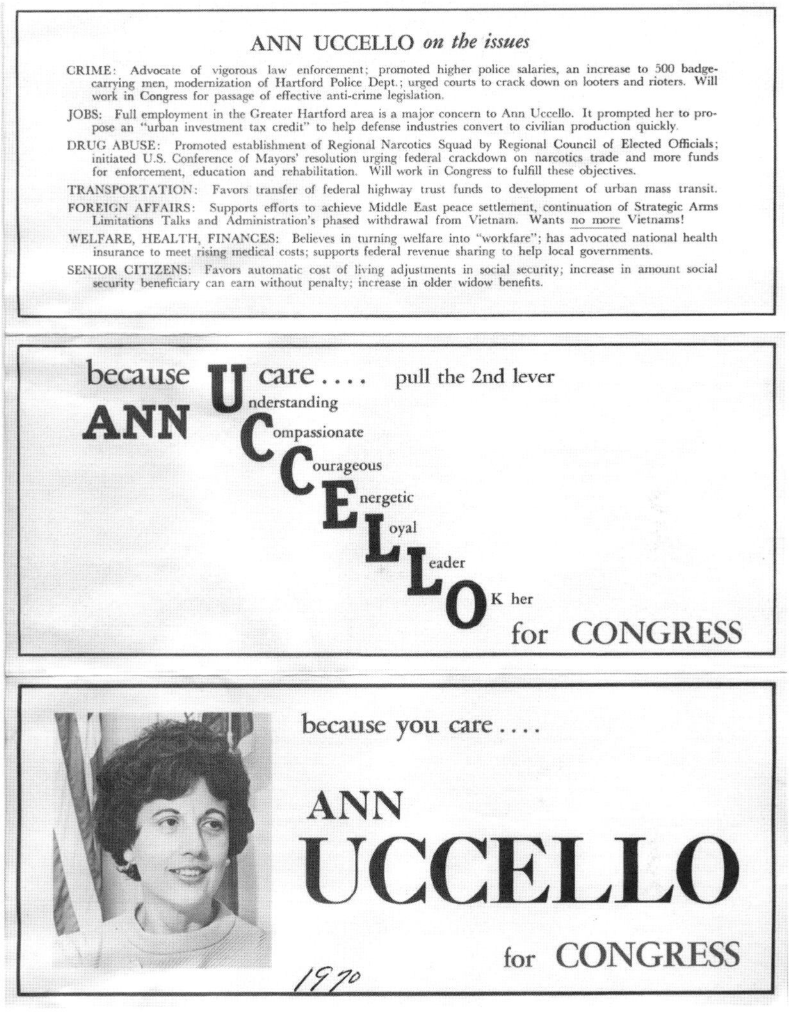

ANN UCCELLO *on the issues*

CRIME: Advocate of vigorous law enforcement; promoted higher police salaries, an increase to 500 badge-carrying men, modernization of Hartford Police Dept.; urged courts to crack down on looters and rioters. Will work in Congress for passage of effective anti-crime legislation.

JOBS: Full employment in the Greater Hartford area is a major concern to Ann Uccello. It prompted her to propose an "urban investment tax credit" to help defense industries convert to civilian production quickly.

DRUG ABUSE: Promoted establishment of Regional Narcotics Squad by Regional Council of Elected Officials; initiated U.S. Conference of Mayors' resolution urging federal crackdown on narcotics trade and more funds for enforcement, education and rehabilitation. Will work in Congress to fulfill these objectives.

TRANSPORTATION: Favors transfer of federal highway trust funds to development of urban mass transit.

FOREIGN AFFAIRS: Supports efforts to achieve Middle East peace settlement, continuation of Strategic Arms Limitations Talks and Administration's phased withdrawal from Vietnam. Wants no more Vietnams!

WELFARE, HEALTH, FINANCES: Believes in turning welfare into "workfare"; has advocated national health insurance to meet rising medical costs; supports federal revenue sharing to help local governments.

SENIOR CITIZENS: Favors automatic cost of living adjustments in social security; increase in amount social security beneficiary can earn without penalty; increase in older widow benefits.

because U care.... pull the 2nd lever
ANN
Understanding
Compassionate
Courageous
Energetic
Loyal
Leader
OK her
for CONGRESS
because you care....
ANN
UCCELLO
for CONGRESS
1970

Congressional race campaign literature from 1970. *Ann Uccello's collection.*

who, for sixteen years, had mismanaged state finances and left the state on the brink of bankruptcy.

The congressional race was going to be a close affair. On September 6, 1970, Jack Zaiman wrote a column for the *Courant* titled, "ANN UCCELLO REAL THREAT TO COTTER." By his analysis, Ann needed to have some fourteen thousand voters switch allegiance from their prior support for Daddario and the Democrats to herself and the GOP. And he declared, "Miss Uccello has a chance for a major upset."

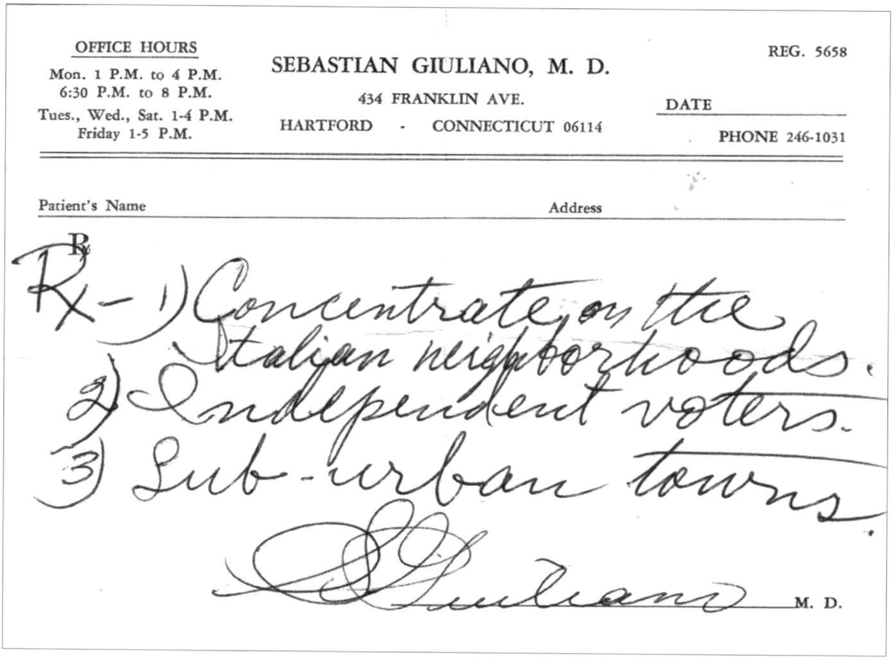

OFFICE HOURS
Mon. 1 P.M. to 4 P.M.
6:30 P.M. to 8 P.M.
Tues., Wed., Sat. 1-4 P.M.
Friday 1-5 P.M.

SEBASTIAN GIULIANO, M. D.
434 FRANKLIN AVE.
HARTFORD - CONNECTICUT 06114

REG. 5658
DATE
PHONE 246-1031

Patient's Name
Address

℞

Rx- 1) Concentrate on the Italian neighborhoods.
2) Independent voters.
3) Sub-urban towns

S. Giuliano M. D.

Ann's mother's doctor sent his own "prescription" for winning in 1970. *Ann Uccello's collection.*

Everybody had a recipe for how to win the congressional seat, including the mayor's parents' doctor, who wrote his own, well, "prescription." The doctor's formula was simple: concentrate on the Italian neighborhoods, independent voters and suburban towns.

The election results were extremely close, but Ann would end up losing by some 1,160 votes. Her normally reliable Hartford support did not come in quite as strong as in prior years. Her concession speech was a mixture of regrets and warnings. She sent a congratulatory note to Representative Cotter but warned that he would hear from her every hour unless he kept his promises. And she reminded gloomy supporters that she was still mayor of Hartford.

The background of the elections paints a picture of a campaign that did not receive the needed support and certainly not the money needed to win a close contest. Nixon came to Hartford that fall to campaign for Meskill, Weicker and Ann, but Meskill and Weicker got to travel with the president while Ann rode with Pat Nixon. These many years later, she still feels strongly that as mayor of Hartford, she should have been in that first limo.

The GOP fundraising efforts in Hartford consisted of a three-candidate event for Meskill, Weicker and Uccello, but that meant she had to share the

Riding the motorcade with Pat Nixon during President Nixon's 1970 visit to Hartford. *Courtesy of the* Hartford Courant.

funds three ways. At the end of that particular event, she made one more trip to the floor than scheduled to make another plea for money.

Ann does not recall much money coming her way from the Nixon GOP. On the day of the election, she received a call from Chuck Colson asking if Ann's campaign could use $5,000 in cash. Ann's reply: "What for, a pizza party?"

George Ducharme, Ann's campaign manager, has a somewhat different recollection. He asked Ann to call Nixon and ask for monetary support. He was sure they would get it, but Ann would not do so. I would not be surprised if this indeed took place. Ann was focused on the issues; she was a policy guru, not someone who would feel confortable asking for money.

The job of mayor has some benefits that a politician appreciates immensily, benefits that break the routine and remind you of why you do what you do and that recharge you. In October 1970, in the midst of a heated congressional campaign, Mayor Uccello made time to meet, greet and have her picture taken with a young girl from Glastonbury. On October 15, 1970, city hall received an envelope addressed to the attention of the mayor containing a priceless letter that did much to cheer Ann.

Every campaign has its conspiracy stories, and this one is no exception. The evidence points to the fact that perhaps there was more to this conspiracy than the simple speculation of a losing candidate looking for excuses for why she lost. George Ducharme was sure that there had been voting irregularities,

WO-HE-LO

54 Brookhaven
Glastonbury, Co
06033

Dear Mayor Uccello,

Thank you so much for inviting me to have my picture taken with you. I am Jane Bonnell, th a Camp Fire Girl who came to your offic on Tuesday to have my picture taken with y And I was delighted! I made a friend, and that friend is you!

And just to thank you for your kindness, your autograph, and your contribution, I shall write a poem to you in your honor, Mayor Uccello,

There's just one mayor that I kno
And that is mayor U-cell-o
I want to tell her what my thoughts are.
She is the nicest person by far

Love,
Jane Bonnell

A 1970 letter to Ann from a young girl who had just visited city hall. *Ann Uccello's collection.*

based on the vote count from some of the districts. He was so sure that right after the election, he and a friend knocked on doors asking if people had voted. His non-scientific approach indicated that a number of people either were out of city or indicated they had not voted, yet the election records indicated otherwise. George turned over the findings to the appropriate authorities, but nothing was ever pursued.

Late in 1969, the International Telephone and Telegraph Company had made a bid to acquire the Hartford Fire Insurance Company, this at a time when acquisitions were rare. The merger required the approval of the state insurance commissioner, Bill Cotter, the same person who would oppose Ann in the congressional election.

In December 1969, Commissioner Cotter had rejected the merger only to reverse his decision in May 1970. In the summer of 1970, the Securities and Exchange Commission had opened an investigation into the approval. The *Hartford Courant* also launched an inquiry into the matter.

The *Courant*, in its wisdom, decided not to publish the story until after the election. The story goes that while it was felt that the reporting was based on facts of interest to the voters, the *Courant* could be accused of running the article to aid Uccello, whom the paper had endorsed.

On November 8, 1970, the *Courant* did publish a front-page article titled "Two Agencies Probing ITT Merger." The article explained that the Justice Department and the Securities and Exchange Commission were looking into four "irregularities" pertaining to the merger:

- The attempting influence of insurance commissioner William Cotter.
- Questionable stock trading before the announcement.
- The uncertain role played by a local Hartford lawyer Joseph Fazzano.
- A secret, unannounced meeting between Cotter and ITT representatives.

Publication of such an article prior to the election would have indeed been a bombshell. Would it have thrown the election to Mayor Uccello? Would it have generated sympathy for Cotter for being attacked at the last minute? We will never know the answers to those questions.

The saga of the ITT–Hartford Fire merger would go on for years. Representative Cotter was never accused of any wrongdoing.

The release of the Nixon White House tapes did rekindle the interest on the issue when it was discovered that, on April 18, 1971, Nixon had placed a phone call to Assistant Attorney General Richard Kleindienst, ordering him in very stern language not to file a brief due the following day in court on the ITT–Hartford Fire merger.

A 1985 column by Don Noel outlines the pros and cons of the *Courant*'s decision in 1970 not to publish information about an SEC investigation of Insurance Commissioner Cotter, who was running for Congress against Mayor Uccello. The mayor lost the election by a mere 1,160 votes, and one could easily argue that the *Courant*'s decision cost Ann the election.

Some forty-two years later, Ann is asking: Did Richard Nixon come to a secret understanding with Harold Geneen, the legendary chairman of ITT, to allow Cotter to win? Is that why no money was sent to Ann's campaign?

The reality of November 1970 was that Ann had, for the first time in her political career, lost an election. She put on a brave face when speaking in front of her supporters, but she was hurting.

Ann now admits that, alone in bed that night, she had a tough time sleeping, and she felt even worse the next morning. She was disappointed, of course, but she was looking for the reasons for the loss, and she was blaming herself for letting down her supporters.

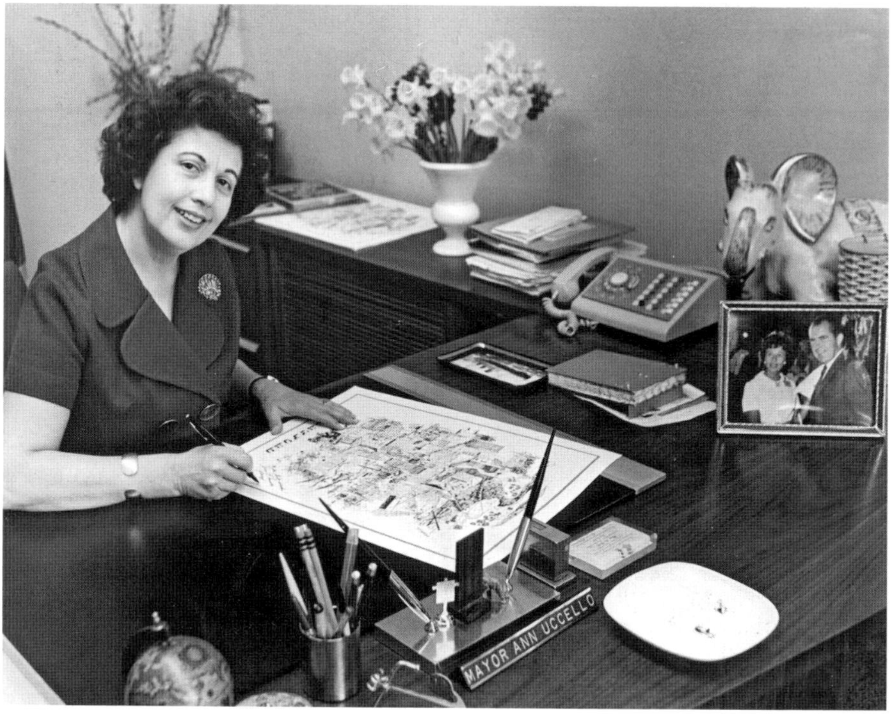

In 1971, the last official day on the job for the mayor before her move to Washington, D.C. *Ann Uccello's collection.*

Transferring lots of paperwork to incoming mayor Athanson. *Ann Uccello's collection.*

Her supporters disagreed, especially the fifth graders from South Windsor, who took time to write to the mayor that they had worked hard for her campaign and that they thought she had been treated roughly by the city voters.

The end of 1970 represented the end of an era in Hartford: it would be the last time, at least for the next dozen years, that Ann Uccello would run for office or be involved in city politics. And almost forty-five years later, she remains the last Republican to hold that office.

"The Mayor Tells It As It Is," read the April 13 editorial in the *Hartford Courant*:

Having valiantly and patiently put up with her share of knocks and frustrations as two-term Mayor of Hartford, it was only fair and natural that Miss Uccello should stand up and say her unimpeded say now that she is departing her post.

Indeed, it was probably her final responsibility in office that she should leave the city a legacy of suggestions and criticisms to chew upon. Certainly municipal government is not that perfect thing above all betterment.

Miss Uccello's prescription for these reported ills is a Strong Mayor, a professional municipal administrator, and a Council enlarged to 21 members nominated on a district basis but elected at large by all the voters.

The city of Hartford has indeed adopted a strong mayor form of government.

In April 1971, Ann was sitting alone in the mayor's office, teary eyed. After four years on the council, four years as mayor and following her very narrow defeat for the First District Congressional seat, she had decided to accept a senior position in the Nixon administration.

After much soul searching, she had reached the decision to go to Washington rather than put the city through another highly partisan election, which was bound to be the case if she had run again. The Democrats, stung by back-to-back losses to a candidate they simply had no answer for, had done their very best to sabotage her performance in office, and they would continue to do so. Even assuming she could win another election (a significant assumption), to what end?

Her competitive spirits would tell her to stay and fight like she had done many times before, not just in politics. She certainly was not happy that her resignation would automatically elevate George Athanson. She was handing the job on a platter to one of her most vocal critics, someone she regarded as not qualified for the position of mayor.

Ann had never aspired to be mayor, and so the tears were not those of someone who sees her prize slipping away but of someone whose life is changing, going in a different direction, and who is not sure what the future would bring.

Her one constant: faith in God and that his will be done.

Chapter 8

The Washington Years

The morning after the loss in the congressional race was a difficult one for Mayor Uccello. For the first time since her meteoric rise to the top of the political world in Hartford, she had lost an election. And having lost by only 1,160 votes made it that much more difficult. She had felt that the prize was within her grasp, and it had gotten away. But why? Had it been the lack of money in the closing days of the campaign? Did Nixon renege on his pledge to provide Ann all the help she would need? Worse yet, did President Nixon withhold funds on purpose so that she would lose to a candidate favored by a business leader close to him? Would she have won the election had the *Courant* published a story about potential irregularities in the approval of the ITT–Hartford Fire merger that had been first rejected and then approved by her opponent, former insurance commissioner Cotter? Had there been widespread voter fraud, as charged by Ann's campaign manager, George Ducharme?

Fortunately, she was still mayor of Hartford, and she had a job to do. She could not afford to spend too much time feeling sorry for herself. The city was facing several difficult issues, and her Democratic opponents were moving in for the kill.

Barely a few days had passed when she received a call from an assistant to President Nixon. The president had instructed this aide to communicate to Mayor Uccello that he wanted her to be part of the administration and identified three departments—Health, Education and Welfare (HEW), run by Secretary Elliot Richardson; Housing and Urban Development (HUD), run by Secretary Romney; and Department of Transportation (DOT), run by Secretary Volpe—as potential places of work.

I asked Ann if this had been discussed before with Nixon, and she commented that never had such an option been discussed before the election, nor had she started a subtle campaign for such a position. Nixon was placing great emphasis on having women in senior administration positions, and she was one who could easily qualify for just about any job.

The press was ripe with speculation as well. Would she be nominated to a senior position within the incoming GOP cabinet of Governor Meskill, who had won the 1970 election? Would she go to Washington? Would she run again in a short two years against Congressman Cotter? Mayor Uccello was never interested in any position on a Meskill administration. The two were never close, and the only official meeting between them, following her joining DOT, lasted but a few minutes and ended with the governor walking her to the door, saying that their few minutes together had come to a close and goodbye.

The next speculation focused on several positions within the Nixon administration. The effort on behalf of Mayor Uccello to get a job in Washington was being spearheaded by Senator Lowell Weicker, who, no doubt, felt a political debt toward Ann for her endorsement of him prior to the convention, for her nominating speech and for the work she did to help Weicker in the city. By the end of March, it was clear that Mayor Uccello would be moving on.

In the meantime, the business of being mayor and running a city took no vacation, and Mayor Uccello had to face the increasingly difficult issues of balancing the effort to maintain the rate of tax mill increase at a reasonable level with the increasingly outlandish requests from the Board of Education for funds.

Over the year, Ann was consistent in her approach to the budget question, and her efforts kept the tax mill under control. But the Board of Education had no such qualms. Its job was to obtain its budget increase, and it was extremely well organized about having its voice heard. The strategy was much the same year after year: the end of the world is coming if the proposed cuts are allowed to stand—or at least hundreds of jobs would be lost and education impaired.

"School Budget Cuts Could Mean Job Loss for 700, Official Says," glared the headline in the *Hartford Courant* on February 16, 1971, followed a few days later by: "GOP Board Members Blast Off at Mayor."

The difference in 1971 was that the GOP council members, led by Margaret Tedone, a former Board of Education member, were the ones leading the attacks on the mayor, a situation that hurt Mayor Uccello as never before. How could the GOP turn so savagely against her, the GOP standard-bearer, their colleague and friend?

When all the dust settled, here is what the February 28, 1971 article in the *Hartford Courant* had to say about the budget battle:

> *School Budget Battle Was Same Old Story*
> *With all of the rhetoric of the past several days, there has been nothing to indicate that anyone in the City would get a better education if Ms. Uccello and the Council would give the Board of Education all that they want… Every year the education administrators and the Board of Education appear to support their campaign for more money with more thumbprints than blueprints…They* [council members] *have perhaps learned of fat administrative salaries; watched the proliferation of new and extravagant schools and wonder why there is so little accountability for all this expense.*

Change the date to 2015, and the issues, unfortunately, are still somewhat the same.

The budget battle was not the only issue Mayor Uccello was confronting and discussing. In a move that clearly angered the police union, she argued for the repeal of the power of police to form bargaining unions, a position for which she received much support. Of course, the police union was not one of those in agreement.

Mayor Uccello also proposed the extremely unpopular step of eliminating longevity payments for city employees. Looking back, one could argue that had those recommendations been accepted, the city finances would look a lot different for the better today.

Launching construction of the Civic Center was her last act as mayor before her announcement that she had accepted a position in Washington.

Mayor Uccello's departure was followed a few days later by the announcement that City Manager Freedman was also resigning, described by the *Courant* as "a double blow to Hartford's Municipal Government" in an editorial on April 14. The move to Washington had not yet happened, but speculation was already starting on when or if Mayor Uccello would ever come back to city or state politics.

Most people who contacted Mayor Uccello about her move were very complimentary and happy for her. She had earned her new position through hard work, and few could match the expertise she had built in her work as mayor.

The year 1971 marked the start of construction of the Hartford Civic Center, the last official act of Mayor Uccello. *Ann Uccello's collection.*

Of course, there is always someone with a different opinion. Ann received a phone call shortly after the announcement that she was leaving. The papers had made a big deal of her new salary, which was a respectable but not eye-popping $32,500. A woman with an Italian surname from the city of Middletown called to yell at the mayor that she was betraying the city by leaving and that all she was interested in was the money while leaving the city to fend for itself.

Ann arrived in Washington on April 12, 1971, and was sworn in by Department of Transportation secretary John Volpe, a former Massachusetts governor and someone who would become the prime supporter and sponsor of Ann's days in D.C.

In April 1971, Ann was invited to the Oval Office for a photo opportunity in which she was met by President Nixon. After some niceties, Nixon walked Ann out of the Oval Office to the Rose Garden and said to her, "You could not steal six hundred votes to win the election?" A semi-stunned Ann almost answered, "But Mr. President, we Republicans don't do things like that," but

Swearing in to her new position at the Department of Transportation in 1971, with Secretary Volpe and Ann's mother. *Official DOT photo.*

Mrs. Volpe, Ann's mother, Secretary Volpe, Ann and Ann's sister Vincenza following the swearing in in 1971. *Official DOT photo.*

At the Oval Office, Ann meets with President Richard Nixon in 1971. *White House photo.*

somehow kept her thoughts to herself and mumbled some routine excuse. As Ann and the country would find out in 1972, '73 and '74, unfortunately, the Nixon political machine at times did that and much more.

Ann did not see much of Nixon but does recall a Christmas party at the White House in December 1971. When she was being introduced by the military aide, President Nixon stepped out of the line, took his famous pose of the hand under his chin and said, "I still think you could have won that election!" Pat Nixon saved the day by complimenting Ann on her dress.

Ann visited the White House only a couple more times. In April 1971, she was invited by Pat Nixon to join her at a meeting with an Italian group from Pennsylvania. She recalls it because she had the fortitude to ask if she could bring her mother, who at the time was staying with her in D.C. Josephine Uccello, the immigrant from Canicattini, a woman who until that time had only traveled outside the United States a couple times, was thrilled that she got to go to a White House reception.

In 1972, Ann was awarded the order of Cavaliere della Repubblica Italiana by Italian ambassador Egidio Ortona at a ceremony at the Italian

In 1972, Ann received the award of Cavaliere della Repubblica Italiana from Italian ambassador Ortona. *Ann Uccello's collection.*

embassy. The recognition was one of the many ways that Ann's Italian heritage was celebrated while she was in D.C.

The relationship with Secretary Volpe was indeed a strong one. He admired Ann's work ethic and smarts, and he was a big supporter of Italian people in general. But Ann had earned her stripes by initiating a process that until that time was not in much use in Washington, D.C.: field hearings to get the input of local officials and citizens about various issues and, in Ann's case, aviation and highway safety.

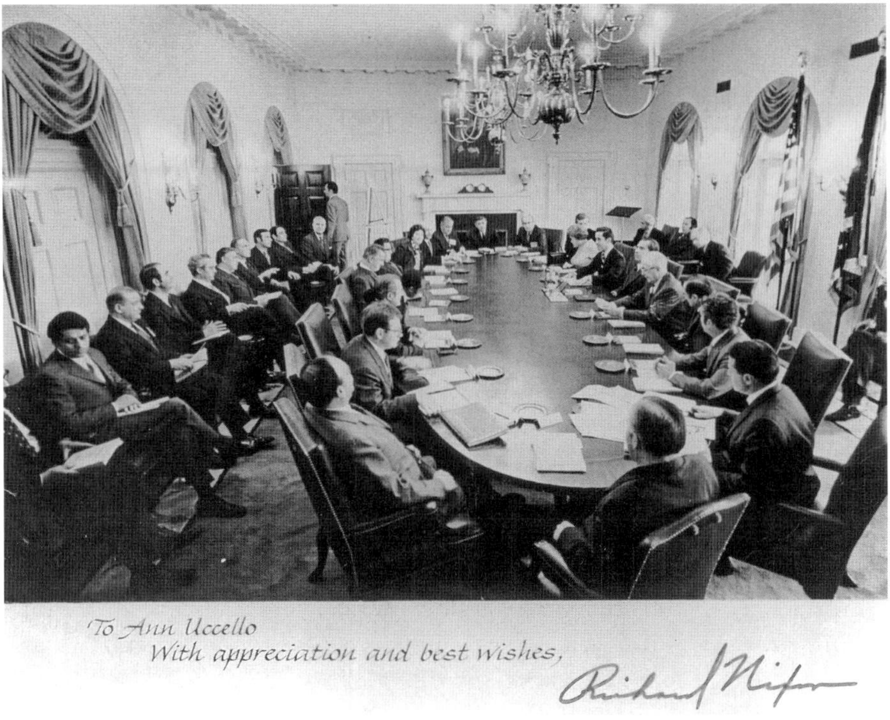
To Ann Uccello
With appreciation and best wishes,
Richard Nixon

Ann (seated at table top left) attends President Nixon's cabinet meeting in 1971. *Official White House photo.*

She was so successful in these events that Secretary Volpe mentioned her activity at a cabinet meeting. Elliot Richardson, then secretary of HEW, called Ann's counterpart at HEW and told him to call Ann, find out what she was doing and do the same thing.

As enjoyable as it was living in Washington, especially with the many perks that came with it (Ann was allowed to dine in the restaurant usually reserved for the secretary and higher positions, and she had a car at her disposal although she would rarely use it, preferring to ride the bus), it was also a challenge.

Ann had rented an apartment and would later purchase a co-op at The Westchester, a prestigious complex on Cathedral Avenue and home to some very famous residents like Barry Goldwater, who apparently was listed as one of her references on the application to the co-op, surely the result of the GOP connections. She would see him only once, on his way back from the pool in a pinkish bathrobe.

But one story towers above all in Ann's mind. She recalls that she went to a local store to purchase the furniture for the co-op. She was met by a salesman, who was thrilled to see Ann point to several pieces, indicating that she wanted to buy them. But just as the salesman may have been counting his commission, Ann came to a devastating realization: she had no money and no credit.

The fellow's face dropped, figuring that he had wasted his time on this deadbeat client. Of course, once the finance person found out who Ann was, her position and background, it was a matter of hours before the entire transaction was successfully finalized, much to the relief of the sales associate.

The co-op became the focal point of many family visits. All the sisters came to visit from time to time, but Vincenza and especially Ann's mother were the most frequent visitors. Eventually, David, Carmela's son, would also spend time there while he was studying at Georgetown University.

John Volpe left in 1973 to become ambassador to Italy while Ann continued to serve in her capacity until August 1977, when the incoming administration of Jimmy Carter eventually asked her to resign but some ten months after most other individuals in similar positions had been let go—another sign of the quality work and lack of politics in Ann's performance.

Ann's time in D.C. was not all work and no play, and she did date a gentleman. They would go out to dinner, they would go out dancing and, on one occasion, Ann accepted an invitation to join this individual in Maryland at a complex he owned. There was only one condition: she wanted her separate apartment. He agreed, and she spent the weekend with him but stayed in their separate places. Ann's values precluded her from acting in any other manner, and her self-imposed vow of celibacy would survive this experience as well.

Back home in Hartford, Ann might have been gone but not forgotten. In 1972, there was speculation of a re-run for the First Congressional District against William Cotter.

Party leaders were surprised in April 1972 when Ann announced that she had decided not to run again for Congress. Her advisers had been split on the question, and money considerations may have weighed as well in her decision. After all, she had experienced those difficulties in the prior campaign, and she was not going to run again unless she was sure of receiving the financial support needed to not only run but also win an election.

The years in Washington were special ones for Ann and perhaps even more so for her mother, who adjusted easily to life in the limelight and would miss D.C. far more than Ann ever did when they returned to Hartford permanently at the end of 1977.

The relationship between Senator Weicker and Ann Uccello may have been the greatest casualty of her years in D.C. Ann recounts an incident when a Greenwich supporter of the senator was traveling in a plane with a dog and conditions were not exactly stellar. The friend complained to the senator, who called in Ann in her position as director of consumer affairs and demanded that she do something and fast. It was not as friendly a conversation as one would expect from two political allies. The senator was very formal and extremely firm with Ann, demanding that she do something or he would call hearings in the Senate. The problem was, not much could be done that fast to accommodate the demands of the senator and his friend. The relationship between the two would never be the same and probably led to Ann's dismissal from a GOP post she would take in 1978 after returning to Connecticut.

Ann made many trips back home to Hartford, as her family was still there. In 1974, the City of Hartford organized the grand opening celebrations of the Civic Center, a project she had launched just before leaving for Washington in 1971. Somehow, she was left off the guest list.

Chapter 9

Second Congressional Race

Ann had lost her job in Washington, and it was time to adjust to life back home, a feat that would prove much easier for her to accomplish than it was for her mother—but more on that later.

In January 1978, Ann accepted a senior position in the state GOP administration as a field coordinator for the First, Second and Sixth Districts, districts clearly Democrats all. But it gave Ann an opportunity to get back in touch with party leaders who would decide any future political candidacy, as well as to get her name back in the press. Columnist Jack Zaiman praised the decision but also stated, "Now she is back resuming her political career in the State. Nobody knows where it will lead, not even Ms. Uccello."

In his column, Mr. Zaiman made one extremely important observation: Ann's victories in Hartford had been personal victories, which everyone pretty much knew, but he then went on to say that she probably lost the election of 1970 to Bill Cotter due to the lack of support from some city GOP leaders who may have sung her praise in public but resented her almost complete independence from the party apparatus. Ann herself had said that she was not a politician, and it would turn out that this factor would lead to both her successes and her failures as a candidate.

In her campaigns, Ann relied very heavily on two key people: George Ducharme and Dick Rittenband. She did not have a political machine, and so she relied very heavily on the volunteers who showed up by the hundreds to distribute flyers and mail postcards, and above all, she relied on her charm. Opponents kept accusing her of not standing on any issues, and in a sense they were right, as she was not an issue-oriented candidate. She relied heavily on the personal qualities of honesty, hard work and intelligence to convince the voters that she would look out for their best interests.

George Ducharme, a self-made campaign manager with no prior political experience but lots of new ideas (he claims most of them came to him in church) and a golden marketing touch, had led Ann to victory, but as George himself told me, he was not welcome at GOP headquarters and was told to stay away during the 1970 campaign for Congress.

Dick Rittenband was a party leader (he himself ran for the First District congressional seat in 1972 and also lost to Bill Cotter), but his role was primarily that of advisor, and he was not sure how much influence he carried at state or city GOP headquarters.

Ann's relationship to Meskill was nonexistent. Gaffney and Hausman, two strong allies of Meskill, treated her more as an opponent and someone to fear as a potential competitor than an ally. Ann recounted an incident that took place at a meeting with Governor Meskill to convince him to support a welfare initiative being introduced by President Nixon. Ann had barely finished speaking when Meskill announced that their time for coffee was over and escorted her out of the room. It was the last time she ever met Governor Meskill.

But above all, the "problem" was Ann herself. I say problem in quotes because it was not a problem per se, but usually candidates have a passion for the political arena, a drive for higher office, a plan for how to achieve their goals. Such was not the case with Ann. She did not have a grand design, and she did not aggressively seek the kind of alliances that, in politics, can make or break a political career. She was not a politician.

By all accounts, Ann did her usual great job and even pulled off a very good upset in the Second District, where a GOP candidate for state representative prevailed in 1978 for the first time in years. She kept busy with some political appearances, but the job was not that fulfilling and certainly a major step down from her days in Washington.

In June 1978, Ann's name was the subject of political speculation for the position of secretary of state. Wallingford city chairman Gregory had started the drive, but it would be very short lived. Ann had expressed her strong dislike for that position before, and she had not changed her mind.

A short six months later, Ann would find herself unemployed once again. Facing a substantial deficit left over by the failed Sarasin campaign for governor, Ann and Fred Biebel, state party chair, reached the conclusion that it was time for Ann to go into the private sector.

Ann's once bright political career had all but disappeared, brought to an end by circumstances and political opponents. In March 1979, Ann joined the Gustafson Agencies (owned by Russ Gustafson, Ann's brother-in-law) as director of sales. It certainly appeared as if that would be the last of Ann Uccello's political life.

In May 1978, Ann was one of three distinguished women to receive the prestigious Alumnae Award from Saint Joseph College. Ann had been an ardent supporter of Saint Joseph from the day after graduation, had made a number of appearances on behalf of the school and had nominated Sister Mary Theodore to a position and fought the council Democrats to make sure she was appointed. And, of course, her sister Vincenza was a professor of fine arts at the college. The ties that linked Ann to Saint Joseph College were strong and long-standing.

Fate has a way of intruding on the best-laid plans, and certainly fate played a major role in Ann's decision to give one more try to the job of First District congressman. In September 1981, Congressman Bill Cotter died at the very young age of fifty-five. Suddenly, there was an opening, and a special election would be held in January 1982 to decide who would replace Mr. Cotter.

Ann would be the first to admit that making a decision to run again for Congress was the worst decision she has ever made in her life. George Ducharme says he was against the decision to run, and so was Dick Rittenband .

Ann's campaign manager was a political operative from Massachusetts by the name of Joseph Malone. The campaign was a difficult one.

Much was made of her opposition to the Equal Rights Amendment, a proposed constitutional amendment designed to guarantee the same rights to women as to men. The amendment had been approved by both houses of Congress and was later approved by thirty-five states, although five would rescind their approval. Congress passed an extension to allow states to approve the amendment, but the effort failed.

Here was Ann Uccello, the daughter of immigrants and the first female mayor in Hartford and in the state of Connecticut, and yet people were questioning her commitment to women rights.

Also controversial and certainly a position that cost her a lot of votes was her opposition to abortion, even in the cases of rape or incest. Not that she regrets her opposition, but that was the position of the church and so it was Ann's position. She recalled getting a letter from a group of nurses from a local hospital informing her that they were ready to support her until her pronouncement on the abortion issue.

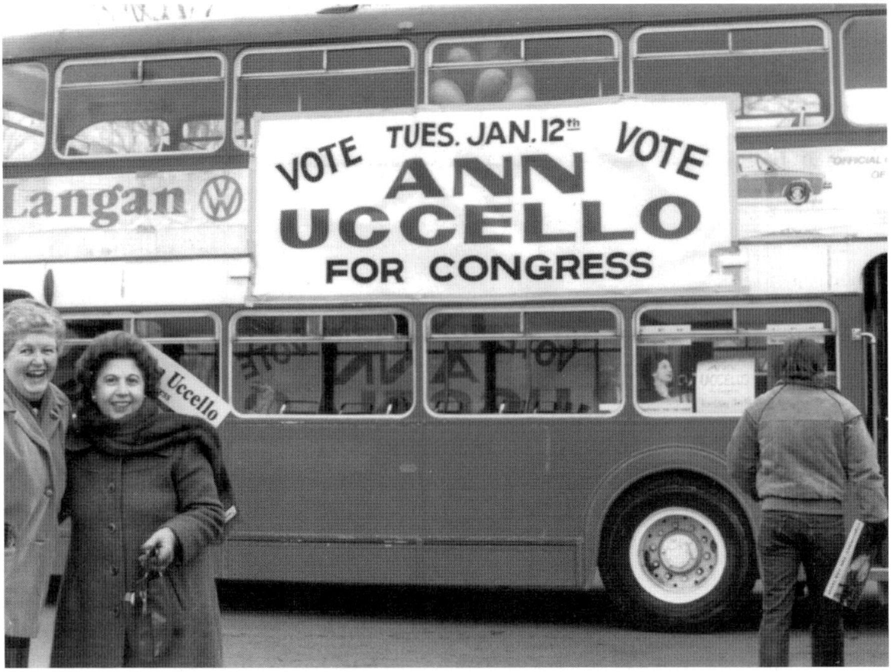

Ann's second congressional campaign in 1981. *Ann Uccello's collection.*

Ann received the GOP endorsement but had to compete in a primary against Coleen Howe (wife of the legendary hockey superstar Gordie Howe), and in December 1981, she beat Mrs. Howe handily. Now she was facing a formidable opponent in Barbara Kennelly, daughter of legendary national Democratic Party chair and the secretary of state.

Neither candidate impressed the press much, but at the end of the day, Ann's outdated views on some issues made Mrs. Kennelly much more acceptable, and she won the endorsement of the *Courant,* which until that time had supported Ann Uccello in all her campaigns.

And when all the votes were in, Barbara Kennelly was the clear victor with some 58 percent of the vote. The heavily Democratic district pointed in that direction, but Ann ran much less strongly than in the past, winning only in GOP cities.

I asked Ann what was different about this campaign, and she pointed to one aspect of this campaign that she had not encountered in any of her previous campaigns. This time around, people were nasty to her. She recalls one incident when a woman reproached her about not being properly dressed. Ann was a few years older and a few pounds

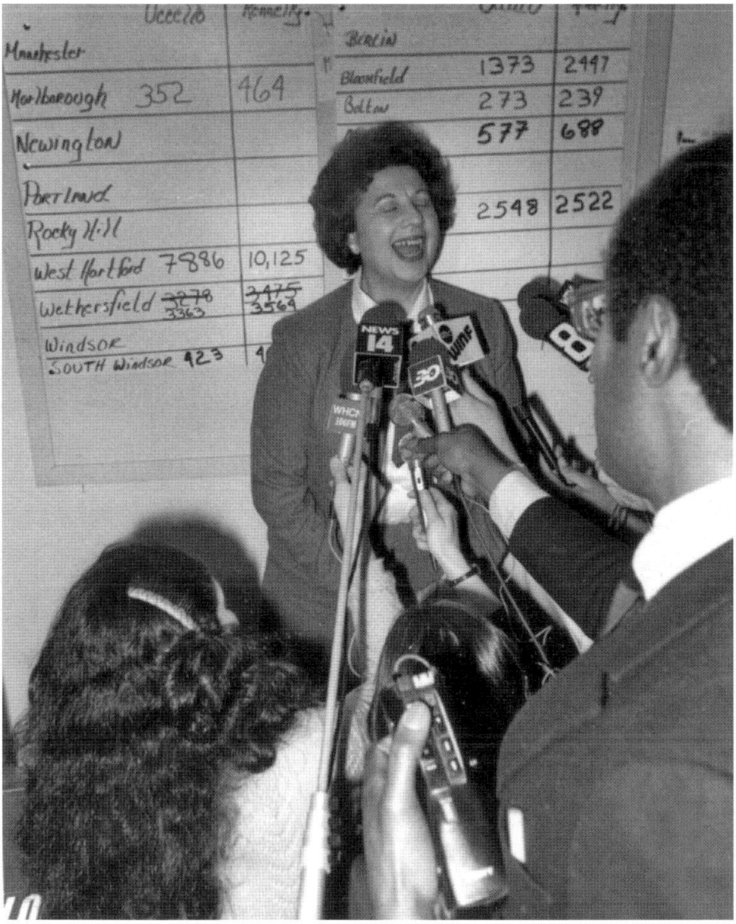

In 1982, Ann concedes the special congressional election to Barbara Kennelly. *Ann Uccello's collection.*

heavier, and she was not the young, fresh face of the 1960s. People were not nearly as kind or accommodating as in prior campaigns.

Not that it took much for Ann to return to her private life. She has the enviable ability to accept what comes, as she believes that God has a plan for her and deals with each situation in a straight-forward manner. She does not believe in looking back and, above all, had no regrets.

Ann Uccello mostly benefited from good press, especially from the *Courant*, while the more liberal *Hartford Times* was much more critical. In my review, I found that Jack Zaiman, *Courant* political columnist, did a particularly good and balanced job in covering Mayor Uccello.

During my research, I came across a column by Dick Polman, *Courant* metro columnist, dated January 9, 1982 (three days before the special congressional election featuring Ms. Uccello against Mrs. Kennelly), that I found rather unfair and biased. In the column, Polman accuses Ann of being ignorant on the issues; of not answering questions; of "stretching her credentials…hear Uccello claim that she made the tough decisions as Mayor of Hartford…even though in April of 1971 she argued that the post of Mayor is devoid of power"; of being appointed to a "specially created patronage job"; and, worst of all sins, of conducting fifty-five hearings around the country but "omitting the fact that not one of those took place in her home state."

Ann would agree on some of those comments. For the first and only time in her political or business career, Ann did not expend the usual hard work to sharpen her message and to learn the details of the issues.

But Mr. Polman made some accusations that I found gratuitous and unfounded, starting with the issue of the "patronage job" Ann had supposedly taken in D.C. Mr. Polman should have known Ralph Nader was the driving force behind the creation of the consumer advocate position within not just the Department of Transportation but also in all federal departments and agencies. And I am sure he would be in favor of such a move if the officeholder had been a Democrat, but a Republican in favor of the consumer—that goes against the narrative.

And Mr. Polman could have easily found out that the position required Ann to be nonpolitical, so not coming to Connecticut was a convenient way to avoid being accused by the press of playing partisan politics. Not to mention that she was already familiar with the state, so why duplicate efforts? And anyway, what does not having held a hearing in Connecticut prove—that she does not care about the state?

But probably no single accusation smacks as more concocted, more unfair, than the one about claiming that she had made tough decisions and then saying that the mayoral jobs did not have power.

Most commentators and the *Courant* editorial board felt and said otherwise. They praised her leadership at a time when she could have coasted by making just social appearances. Compare her four years in office to those of Mayor Athanson, who succeeded Ann in April 1971. The fact is there is no comparison.

Ann operated on the basis of preserving the office of mayor in high esteem. Ann was there during the riots, helmet in hand, in the middle of the burned-out North End, talking to residents and trying to restore the calm.

She did not shy away from pointing out the steps she would take to correct the emerging citywide problem of the middle class leaving the city in droves, and Ann was there to advocate for low-income housing in the North End.

The *Courant* editorial board, much more balanced in its examination of Mayor Uccello's record, makes these points in its editorial quoted below and written just before her departure for Washington.

"To voice a bit of old fashioned sentiment, Washington's gain will be Hartford's loss," the paper declared. It praised her as "federal material" and stated that "she has been active at all times"—competent, hardworking and qualified.

Not to mention that she was the first female mayor in Hartford, in the state of Connecticut, in any capital city of the United States. The daughter of immigrants who raised her to value her faith, her family, hard work and self reliance. Not even a blind person could possibly miss these attributes.

Chapter 10

The Rest of the Story

There are many aspects of the Uccello family that I find remarkable, but none more so than the undying ties to their roots, to a small city in Sicily that was the birthplace of Ann's parents.

In September 2014, as Ann and I were working on this book, I saw Salvo Petruzelli, a young man from Canicattini who was visiting Hartford. I had met Salvo the year before in Canicattini, where I had the opportunity to make a presentation at the local Museum of the Immigrants where Salvo volunteered. Unusual for a young man his age—some twenty-seven years old—Salvo has a real interest in family history. He mentioned to me that he is related to the Uccello family, and so after asking Ann if I could do so, I invited Salvo to join us for a pizza dinner that would be attended by Ann and her sister Nellie; by her sister Carmela; Carmela's husband, Russ; and their two children, Laura and David, with their respective spouses, as well as my wife, mother-in-law and me.

It turned out that Salvo wasn't just some distant cousin with whom the Uccellos had lost contact long ago but rather the son of a close relative whom Ann had met on her many trips to Sicily; whose house she and her mother had stayed in when they were "*o paisi*" (in town); with whom Nellie Agostino (daughter of Salvatore's sister, Lucy, who at age fourteen had left her home city to come to America with the newlyweds Josephine and Salvatore), in many ways the sixth "sister" of the Uccello clan, had been in constant contact via letters and phone calls.

I was really struck by the importance of this relative to the Uccellos, as evidenced by the warm way they greeted him, although many of them had never met him before. It was like they had found a part of themselves that they had lost and that had been missing. It was much more than the routine encounter between us immigrants and visiting cousins with whom we have long ago lost all contacts and attachment. In a way, it speaks to the changes in society, in family structure and in the interaction and support among family members.

Ann recounted how just about the only time that she heard her parents argue was about Salvatore's constant wish to send monetary and other in-kind help to relatives back home. Not that Josephine was not herself very generous and wanting to help, but with five girls to support, she felt that charity begins at home. After all, it wasn't as if they were that well off.

The Uccello family that Salvatore had left behind was very poor, and that had driven Salvatore, the eldest of seven children who survived (three girls died early on), to come to America. So he knew very well what conditions were like back home and felt a moral obligation to help.

Salvo indicated to me that the help was indeed a godsend, as recounted by his grandfather and Uccello first cousin Pasqualino. This help was so desperately needed that they even received either money or the material for the wedding dress of one of the daughters from America.

Nor did the death of Salvatore in 1969 lessen the ties to Sicily. In 1973, Ann, Vin, Josephine and a young David (Carmela's son) traveled to Italy and spent some time in Canicattini. Josephine stayed back for several weeks while Ann, Vin and David toured Italy. Later on, Nellie and her husband, Steve, joined Josephine in Canicattini, and they all returned to America together.

In 1983, Ann took Laura, Carmela's daughter who had just graduated from college, to Canicattini, and again they stayed with the same relatives as in 1973. But over the years, it was Nellie Agostino who would write, call and visit most often and would serve as intermediary, making sure that news of births, deaths, weddings and other family occasions would be shared with the relatives in Canicattini.

I seriously doubt we will see such close-knit families ever again. These family members were tied together by blood, by need, by family structure. Today, we prefer privacy and independence, whereas yesterday they prized interdependence and extended families.

Ann did have one major distraction during her last political campaign: her mother's health continued to deteriorate. Josephine had become accustomed to the spotlight in D.C. She had spent a life playing a supporting role to the needs of her husband and their five daughters, which, after all, was what she had grown up believing in. After the death of Salvatore in 1969, some forty-nine years after their marriage, she had the support of Ann and Vincenza, who continued to live with her.

The stint in Washington was the only period she had devoted time to herself: she would be rubbing elbows with the highest leaders in the country, going to the Kennedy Center for shows, once even attending a reception at the White House with Mrs. Nixon and Ann to greet an Italian group of women from Pennsylvania.

How could she not be impressed, and how could she not love it? Washington, D.C., was about as far, both physically and intellectually, from her upbringing as can be imagined. Her outgoing personality and flair for performance (she loved to sing opera arias at home, and she was always the center of conversation and the jokester) fit in well in D.C.

Now it was back home to the boring, familiar and repetitive routine of daily life, and although she would be closer to all of her daughters and relatives, she dearly missed those few fleeting weeks spent in D.C.

Upon returning home, Josephine's conditions continued to worsen. She became depressed, and she suffered from back and stomach pains. She would pass entire days lying on the sofa and had lost all desire to cook, unimaginable for a woman whose invitation to a home-cooked dinner was more desirable to so many than dating one of the five girls.

The feisty woman had been the life of the party and unafraid to speak her mind—such as the time in 1980 when she decided to unilaterally "revise" the invoice she had received from an appliance supplier because they were not moving fast enough to respond to her requests.

Ann and her sister Vincenza took turns taking her to see various doctors and even took her to a psychiatrist without telling her so. After the visit, she gave them an angry look and said, "*Ora macari pazza mi piggiati*" (now you even think that I am crazy).

In 1984, Ann and her sisters decided the time had come to place their mother, now eighty-four years old, in a convalescent home. They took her to a place in Newington, and much to their surprise, she found herself at home and agreed to stay there on what was to be a "temporary" move until she got better. Later, she would move to Hughes Convalescent Home in West Hartford.

The move did help Josephine by placing her in an environment with people, whereas at home she would spend the day alone since both Ann and Vin were working. She even confided to Ann that some fellow was trying to "seduce" her. But, "*maritu ci n'e' unu sulu,*" there is only one husband, she said, explaining why she could never accept such a proposition.

Over the almost dozen years that Josephine spent in a convalescent home, Ann would perform the role of key caretaker. Vincenza was busy at her college, while Carmela, Gil and Nellie had their own families to tend to. There was not a week that ever went by without the sisters checking in on their mother, but Ann would spend five days a week visiting with her mother. Ann's work schedule (she was working for her brother-in-law Russ Gustafson) allowed her the flexibility to accommodate her mother's needs, and she would usually be at the convalescent home by 3:00 p.m., and if she was late, her mother would call to find out why she was late, at least during the first few years when she retained her full mental capabilities.

Josephine would never return home. She died in 1995, just days short of her ninety-fifth birthday.

Nellie Agostino, daughter of Salvatore's sister, requested and was granted her wish to write and deliver the eulogy. While this may seem somewhat odd, it must be remembered that Lucy, Salvatore's sister and Nellie Agostino's mother, had come to the States with Salvatore and Josephine in 1920. A few years younger than Josephine, Lucy lived with the Uccellos. She helped manage the family and take care of the young girls. That closeness never wavered after Lucy's wedding to Paul Agostino nor after their two children, Nellie and Sam, were born. Nellie was like a sixth sister to the five Uccello girls, and they would see one another just about every day and spend holidays together. They are close to this day. Nellie also attended Saint Joseph and graduated in 1949. In 1983, she received the Distinguished Alumna Award.

It is fair to say the Uccello and Agostino families were a lot closer than the families of the four Uccello brothers. Antonio lived in East Hartford and was also a shoemaker, Santo lived mostly in Manchester and operated a beauty parlor and Giuseppe was in New York. Antonino was the most conservative and tried to persuade Ann to give up her race for mayor in 1969, when Salvatore died in the middle of the campaign. The brothers themselves were in constant contact, but the overall families were not.

Lucy died at the very young age of fifty-nine in 1964, while the brothers died in 1977 (Santo), 1987 (Joseph) and 1990 (Antonio).

Ann and Vin continued to live together, although they moved first to Newington and then to West Hartford and within West Hartford while Carmela and Russ lived in Avon, Nellie and Steve in Wethersfield and Gil and Al in Easton.

Vin's life was dedicated to her two loves: the arts and Saint Joseph. She worked until age eighty-one. She organized exhibits. She painted and produced other works. She taught. She traveled. And she shared her home with Ann, two committed singles and soul mates.

For over thirty-eight years, Vincenza devoted her time and talents to bringing the world of art into the lives of all the members of the Saint Joseph College Community and beyond.

Vincenza belonged to many professional organizations and was a past president of the Connecticut Women's Artists Association. She passed away in 2004 after a brief illness.

Ann recounts how starting a couple years before her death, Vin began to express the desire to be buried at Cedar Hill Cemetery in Hartford and not at the family burial site, located at Mount Saint Benedict in Bloomfield. Ann forgot the conversation, but some months later, Vin again raised the issue, and this time she informed Ann that she was not talking about just the two of them but also wanted to exhume her parents' bodies and move them to Cedar Hill. And, a stunned Ann was informed, the cost would be $3,000 per person, but they would need to obtain the permission of the archbishop of Hartford.

Several weeks before Vin's death, Ann arranged a visit to Cedar Hill and purchased two plots. Upon returning to the hospital, she told her sister, then bedridden and sickly, what she had done. Vinnie raised one finger—one plot? When Ann told her that she had purchased two plots, Vin broke into one of the happiest, most peaceful smiles Ann had ever seen from her sister.

Vincenza was by far the closest sister to Ann, both in age and in spirit. They lived together, either with their parents or by themselves, for decades. They were there for each other when things did not work out as expected. In 1999, Vin was instrumental in getting Ann recognized by the Connecticut Women's Hall of Fame. Unbelievable as it may seem, this organization somehow had overlooked Antonina "Ann" Uccello, first female mayor of Hartford, first female mayor in Connecticut, first female mayor of a capital city in the country and senior member of the Nixon administration. Vincenza made sure they found out about Ann by submitting a thick binder covering Ann's life from graduation at Saint Joseph to her political accomplishments. The board, in its wisdom, decided that Ann did deserve a place in its Hall of Fame, and in 1999, she was inducted.

Following Vincenza's death, Ann decided to move to an independent living facility, but one of her sister's most complex works of art hangs in Ann's bedroom—a constant reminder, if one was needed, of their lives together.

Over the past few years, with Ann getting less mobile, David, the firstborn of Carmela Uccello and Russ Gustafson, has taken over a lot of the family duties. David was a special child, the "gift" that Ann's father had wanted so much: a male member of the family. And Nonno would be proud indeed of the man David has grown to be.

Carmela, David and Russ moved into the first floor of the Uccello two-family home on Blue Hills Avenue in 1956. Vincenza, Ann, Nellie and Virgilia lived upstairs with their parents. Needless to say, David was the center of attention and the object of so much love from the entire extended family. The Gustafson family lived there until 1963, when they moved to Avon. In 1961, Carmela and Russ welcomed the arrival of a baby girl, Laura.

During those early years, David would spend considerable time at the home of his grandparents, who had moved to Branford Street in 1957. Perhaps that is why he has shown so much attachment to his roots, why he has become the fiercest proponent of his aunt and her accomplishments and why, some fifty-plus years later, David has become the head of the family that he loves so much and to which he devotes so much of his time and attention.

David also spent several years in Washington, D.C., at first attending Georgetown University, and then he remained in D.C. until the mid-1980s. He roomed with Aunt Ann, and even after Ann returned to Hartford in 1977, she helped by letting David stay in the condo she owned.

David also is the only Uccello heir to have dipped his feet in politics, although never in an elected position. He worked on several political campaigns, especially the Reagan 1980 presidential campaign, and actually received a personal phone call of thanks from the president elect. In 1983, he was appointed to a position in the Department of Housing and Urban Development, where he served until 1987, when he returned home to manage the insurance business his father had founded in 1956 and where Ann also spent years working until her retirement in 2004. David's commitment to the family, his interest in public service and his core values were all influenced and strengthened by Ann's example and accomplishments.

Over the past several years, there appears to have been a revival of the history of the first female mayor of Hartford and perhaps a greater appreciation of what she accomplished and her contribution to the city she loves. In 2008, Hartford mayor Eddie Perez did the honors in changing a street name from Ann Street to Ann Uccello Street. It was a

Ann and her sisters in their last photo together in 2004. Vincenza died a month later. *Ann Uccello's collection.*

small token of appreciation on the part of a grateful city to one of its most important leaders.

The ball may have been placed in motion by a *Hartford Courant* editorial dated December 4, 2007, and titled "Exceptional Miss Uccello," celebrating the fortieth anniversary of her becoming the first female mayor.

Ann is not sure how it got started, but a committee was formed to come up with an appropriate way to honor Ann's achievements. The first alternative was to name the fountains in front of city hall after Ann in honor of her efforts to get the water running again in those same fountains by organizing the Fountain Balls to raise money for the project. Another idea called for a statue to be built, but Ann rejected that idea out of hand.

Ann was not supposed to have known about the efforts to honor her, but she did find out from David. She suggested the idea of naming a street after her—specifically Ann Street, which was so dear to her from her days as a youthful schoolgirl and her days working at G. Fox. The committee agreed, and so was born Ann Uccello Street.

In 2012, current Hartford mayor Pedro Segarra presented Ann with the key to the city on the occasion of her ninetieth birthday.

On May 19, 2012, the *Hartford Courant* published an editorial under the title "A Daughter of the City":

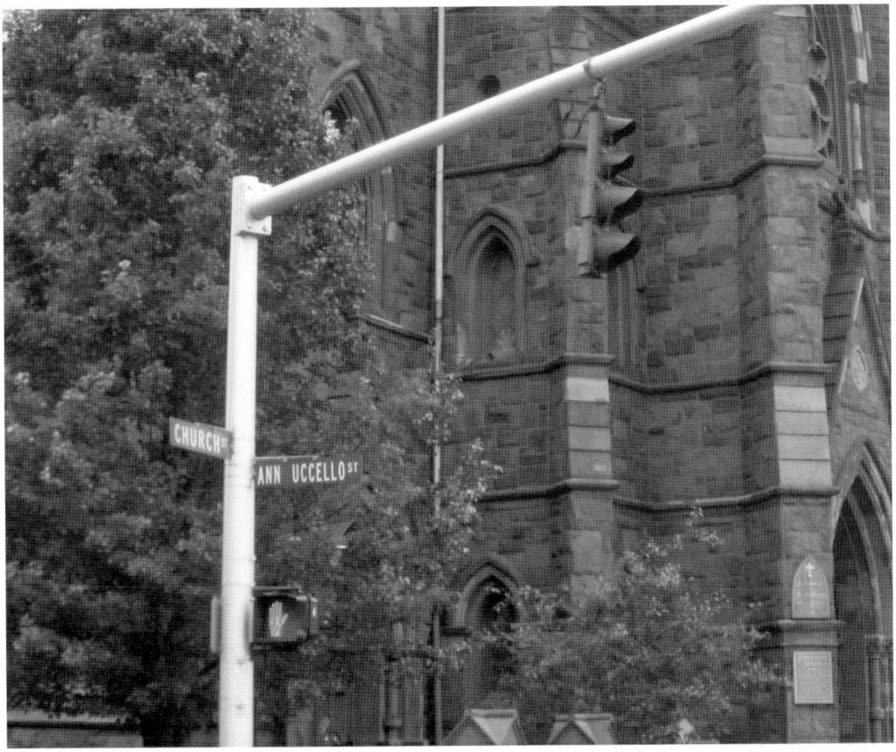

Ann Uccello Street was officially renamed in 2008. *Ann Uccello's collection.*

As the story goes, the young executive at G. Fox went to her boss, Beatrice Fox Auerbach, in 1963 and said she'd like to run for Hartford city council. Since the council met on Mondays, a day the famed department store was closed, Mrs. A gave her blessing.

What followed was one of the most remarkable—if all too brief—political careers in Hartford history. The woman was Ann Uccello, a daughter of Italian immigrants and a Republican. She served two terms on the council before being elected mayor in 1967—a remarkable accomplishment for a Republican in a heavily Democratic city (she remains the city's last Republican mayor). Indeed, she was the first woman to serve as mayor of a capital city in the country.

Intelligent, courageous, graceful under pressure, Ms. Uccello, as the newspapers always called her, championed better housing, job training and protecting children from lead paint, among other things.

In October 2013, the mayor of Canicattini Bagni, Mayor Amenta, came calling on Ann to show his appreciation for all that she had accomplished, as well as to convey the love and respect of her parents' home city's residents and her relatives.

Epilogue

Mayor Ann was not a politician. Her youthful looks, no doubt, helped her win elections, but it was her hard work and ethical behavior that defined her and endeared her to the electorate, not just the image.

Antonina "Ann" Uccello was the first compassionate conservative. Driven by her Catholic faith, by the family experience during the Depression era and by the core values instilled in her by a strong father, Ann was pragmatic and preached self-reliance but also recognized that government must play a role in the life of its citizens. She advocated the construction and rehabilitation of low-income housing but argued for cuts on the bloated education budget. She supported equal rights but took a tough "law and order" position on the 1969 riots. She warned the suburbs, long before Nick Carbone but in a language less confrontational and incendiary, that the city role in the life of suburbs and its residents required a closer working relationship and additional support. And she argued that the high tax rates of the city were driving out more and more middle-income families, leaving a city more and more with a concentration of low-income and minority families. Unfortunately, she has been proven correct in those predictions.

Not being a politician was both an asset and a liability. The voters loved her independence, but her fellow politicians and especially party leaders resented it. The victories Ann scored from 1963 to 1969 were very much personal victories, and her GOP colleagues would not benefit from any coattails. Ann was a political loner. George Ducharme, her campaign manager until 1970, and Dick Rittenband, her trusted advisor, were her strongest supporters, but her relationship with each allowed them to get only so close. Ann did not realize until recently, more than almost fifty years later, that George had quit his job at G. Fox in order to devote his full attention to her political career for almost six years.

During our many conversations in the preparation of this book, Ann herself expressed the view that she was handicapped by not having a husband, a man on her side with his own connections to be leveraged for her political career and with whom she would be able to share and discuss her deepest thoughts, fears and aspirations. No event probably better illustrates this situation than the 1970 decision to run for the First Congressional District. She was outmaneuvered at every turn by her GOP male politicians and pushed into accepting a challenge she had not sought. She wanted to run for Senate but had doubts about the depth of knowledge of the issues. She really wanted to run for governor, and polls back then indicated she was an extremely well-recognized and popular figure who could have possibly run and won.

The lack of a real political inner circle, the limited influence with GOP party leaders and the lack of a partner who could encourage her all worked to curtail a political career that could have shone even brighter and could have prevented Ann—in perhaps the only decision she regrets making—from attempting an impossible comeback much too long after her name had disappeared from the local political scene.

Ann's faith (and her sister Vincenza) have been the constant companions in her entire life. She holds no grudges, and she does not express any hate toward her political rivals, Democrats or Republicans. She burst into a huge laugh when I told her that I had recently run into former Democratic town councilman and leader Nick Carbone. When I told him that I was writing a book about Ann, he asked me to tell her that "Nick the knife" says hello. That is what Ann used to call Nick when she, as mayor, and Carbone, as councilman, often would argue about issues.

She loves Hartford, her home city, and like many is concerned about the direction of the city and about the lack of progress over the last fifty years to fix the core issues.

Ann is one of a kind, and she fits no precast role or mold. She is a trail blazer, committed to fairness and justice, and she is a child of the Depression who worries about today's excessive consumerism.

Ann's contribution to the women's movement has been overlooked and minimized by those who differ from her conservative political views. In a way, she was exactly the type of woman that the feminists were idealizing:

independent, not afraid to take on the good old boys' network, a tough woman who did not shy away from heated discussions and a strong hands-on leader who stepped into the streets of Hartford in the midst of the worse riots this city had ever seen. Ann fiercely advocated the right of women to equal opportunities and access to education, a view that her parents had instilled in her long ago and which was largely responsible for her accomplishments.

Ann's ties to the homeland of her parents are still remarkably strong. I recently went back to Canicattini to open an exhibition on the life of Ann Uccello, and her nephew David, Carmela's son, joined us to represent the family. Her paternal relatives still live in the same house, and therefore it was not difficult to reestablish contact, but the ties to her mother's side of the family had been lost.

Before David left, Ann dug out a postcard she had received from relatives on her mother's side of the family many years earlier and asked David to see if he could find them. We did, and with the aid of a translator friend, we were able to arrange an emotional meeting during which the relatives placed a phone call to Ann that brought tears to all.

The values that Ann learned and practiced her entire life come from there, from a small town in the southeastern part of Sicily at a time when people did not know they were poor and enjoyed the strong family ties that overcome all difficulties.

Ann has never been one to look back and overanalyze her every move to see what she should have done different or better. She lives in the present and not in the past. However, being human, there are those moments when she will ask herself: "What did I really accomplish"?

The answer came in the form of a letter Ann received in 1993. Ann's mother had been ill and in the hospital and was sharing the room with another woman, Italian American as well. Both women recovered nicely, but the husband of the other patient died shortly thereafter, and Ann sent a note of condolences to the family.

In return, she received a letter from the family, written by the dead man's daughter, which in a way not at all expected provided the answer to the question that Ann would consider from time to time—i.e., her legacy.

Here is an excerpt of the salient passages from the letter.

> *It's funny how things come full circle sometimes. My dad was a sweet and gentle man who had a fierce pride in his heritage. When we lived in Hartford, he almost burst when you were elected Mayor. He was so delighted he even overlooked his old-fashioned thinking and admitted a*

> *woman could do a good job. Thanks to your wonderful example he finally admitted it was ok for me to go to college. And become someone like Ann Uccello…I was always grateful to you because you overcame ignorance and opened doors for me just by being yourself.*
>
> *To my dad you were an Italian-American heroine. To me you were someone who could be a success on her own merit, without resorting to the radical feminism which was all around me and with which I couldn't identify. I understood the good old fashioned values you exemplified because I shared them and knew they were at the core of my being. I didn't have to change who I was or deny my principles to get there.*
>
> *For fifteen years I enjoyed a good career in labor relations: I owe it all to you.*

Antonina "Ann" Uccello was a conservative and religious woman who, in the midst of the 1960s women's lib movement, did not have to change her values to pursue a career. She is truly a trailblazer.

Bibliography

Ducharme, George. Personal interview, 2014.

Gustafson, David. Personal interviews, 2014–15.

Hartford Courant, 1963–2012.

Hartford Times, 1963–71.

Rittenband, Richard. Personal interview, 2014.

Uccello, Ann. Papers and letters.

———. Personal interviews, 2014–15.

Uccello, Nellie Romaine. Personal interview, 2014

Index

H

I

K

L

M

N

O

P

R

S

T

U

V

W

Z

About the Author

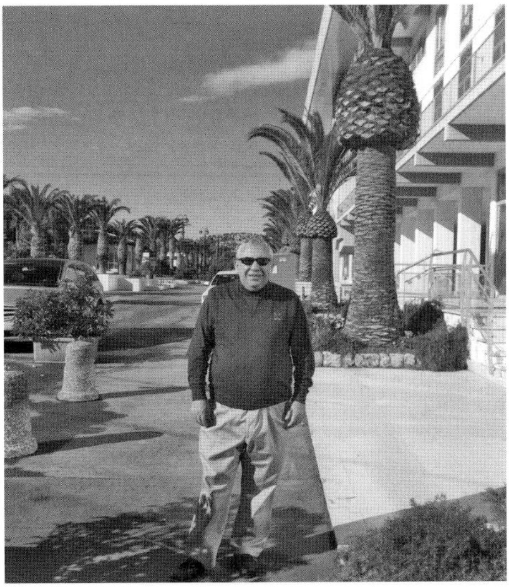

A 1970 graduate of the Istituto Tecnico A. Rizza in Siracusa, Italy, Paul Pirrotta immigrated to the United States in 1970 and established a residence in Connecticut, where he obtained both a bachelor of science degree in business administration and a master's in business administration in international business from Central Connecticut State University.

He began a successful banking career in 1972 and worked in the international banking arena for large New England banks, serving the global financial needs of local importers, exporters and foreign direct investment firms based in New England, until his retirement. He has traveled to and done business in over forty countries, and his efforts have been recognized both at the national and local levels (Ex-Im Bank Small Business Bank of the Year in 2000 while at Webster Bank and Metro Hartford International Business Leader of the Year in 2001). He has served on many boards, including the Sub-Sahara Africa Ex-Im Bank Advisory Board, the Connecticut District

Export Council, the Connecticut World Affairs Council and CIBER at the University of Connecticut.

In 2009, he published *From Sicily to Connecticut*, and in 2015, he published the same book in Italian. For a period of two years, he was a guest columnist for the *Hartford Business Journal*, writing on international trade and finance issues.

In 2012, he founded Casa Emigranti Italiani and created its related website, http://casa-emigranti-italiani.org/our_story/paul_pirrotta, designed to research and document the history of Italian immigrants in the Hartford area. As executive director of Casa Emigranti, he has organized pictorial exhibits on Italian immigration in 2014 in cooperation with the City of Hartford and in March 2015 in cooperation with Central Connecticut State University. In April 2015, he organized an exhibition on former Hartford mayor Ann Uccello in her parents' hometown of Canicattini Bagni.